PORTFOLIO / PENGUIN

DIE EMPTY

TODD HENRY is the founder of Accidental Creative, a consultancy that helps people and organizations generate brilliant ideas. His books have been translated into more than a dozen languages, and he is a sought-after speaker on creativity, productivity, leadership, and passion for work. Visit www.ToddHenry.com to learn more.

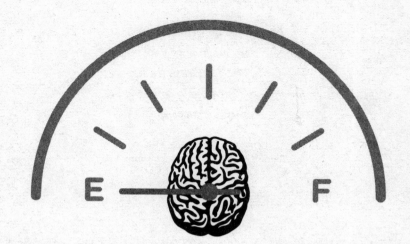

DIE EMPTY

UNLEASH YOUR BEST WORK EVERY DAY

TODD HENRY

PORTFOLIO / PENGUIN

For my father, Mike Henry,
for showing me how to take risks;
for my friend Brian Tome,
for showing me how to bend my life
around a mission.

PORTFOLIO / PENGUIN
Published by the Penguin Group
Penguin Group (USA) LLC
375 Hudson Street
New York, New York 10014

USA | Canada | UK | Ireland | Australia | New Zealand | India | South Africa | China
penguin.com
A Penguin Random House Company

First published in the United States of America by
Portfolio / Penguin, a member of Penguin Group (USA) LLC, 2013
This paperback edition with a new preface published 2015

THE LIBRARY OF CONGRESS HAS CATALOGED THE HARDCOVER EDITION AS FOLLOWS:
Henry, Todd.
Die empty: unleash your best work every day / Todd Henry.
pages cm
Includes bibliographical references and index.
ISBN 978-1-59184-589-8 (hc.)
ISBN 978-1-59184-699-4 (pbk.)
1. Job satisfaction.   2. Employee motivation.   3. Quality of work life.   I. Title.
HF5549.5.J63H37 2013
650.1—dc23   2013019035

Printed in the United States of America
9   10   8

Set in ITC New Baskerville Std
Designed by Alissa Amell

CONTENTS

PREFACE TO THE PAPERBACK EDITION

How much work did you do today that you will be proud of tomorrow? I don't mean just how you handled the big things, but also how you addressed the little, seemingly insignificant ones. Did you make progress on what matters most to you, or did you allow the buzz, busyness, and expectations of others to squelch your passion and focus?

I've been asking these questions of others and myself each day for more than a decade, and they are the main reason I originally felt compelled to write *Die Empty*. Through my work I've encountered many teams of brilliant, sharp, amazing, talented people who have at some point "settled in" or begun coasting on past success. Unfortunately, this often leads to deep regrets. It's not that these people aren't getting things done; perhaps they are even succeeding in the marketplace. It's that in "settling in" they are ignoring the small hunches, ideas, and bits of intuition that could lead to something truly remarkable. For this reason, many of us have had to sacrifice long-term greatness on the altar of short-term efficiency. We have stopped unleashing our best work each day.

Unleashing your best work means ensuring that your daily mix of work includes the important work that you *should* be doing for yourself (but may have been ignoring) in addition to the work that you *must* do as a function of your job.

Your best work may include choosing to have the difficult conversations you've been deferring, setting aside time to invest in future results rather than just focusing on immediate outcomes, and pushing yourself out of your comfort zone in order to learn a new skill or sharpen your thinking. In short, it means choosing not to defer your contribution, but instead working with urgency and diligence each day as you make progress on building a body of work that represents your real values, hopes, and ambitions. It's about putting your focus, assets, time, and energy into the work that matters most. Your *best* work.

I have learned that there are no clear rules for success, but I believe there is enough evidence to make this claim: a person who intentionally structures work and life around what matters most to them will find a greater degree of gratification and will ultimately produce better results than those who don't. Unfortunately, our culture often doesn't provide for this kind of fulfillment. We spend more time trying to find easy roads to success or comparing our career paths to those of others rather than striving to maximize our contribution in our own areas of influence. It's clear that a significant share of the energy expended by employees is spent playing politics or clamoring for the next promotion. Many have lowered their sights from working toward the long-term goals of their organization to the short-term gratification they might be able to achieve as individuals. Even those who came in bright-eyed and optimistic have become worn by short-term thinking and eventually settle into the fold.

The good news is that we all have the ability to shun mediocrity and can instead live and work by design. If you refuse to settle, then there has never been a more opportune time for you to build a remarkable body of work. The current marketplace

might have job uncertainty, but the upside is that it's now necessary to take your career into your own hands. You can no longer
count on your company, your manager, or your industry to define your next steps. Instead, you must stay diligent and alert
and plot your own course. Opportunity abounds for those who
are willing to step into the heart of uncertainty, find their voice,
and commit themselves to battles worth fighting. Now more
than ever, we are each accountable for plotting our own path.

George Bernard Shaw once wrote, "I want to be thoroughly
used up when I die, for the harder I work the more I live. I re-
joice in life for its own sake. Life is no 'brief candle' to me. It is sort
of a splendid torch which I have got hold of for the moment,
and I want to make it burn as brightly as possible before hand-
ing it on to future generations." I believe that the most gratifying
life you can live is one that's committed to ideals that go beyond
your own comfort and enjoyment. This doesn't mean living a life
of martyrdom or always shunning pleasure. Rather, it means that
to build a remarkable body of work you must commit to doing
the right thing even when it's uncomfortable and to emptying
yourself every day rather than deferring action. Since *Die Empty*
was published, I've received countless e-mails from artists, managers, entrepreneurs, writers, and others expressing that they have
adopted the ideal of emptying themselves and acting on what
matters most each day. My wish for you is that you will muster
the same courage and take action today on the things that you've
been holding back. Unleash your best work, and refuse to take
it to the grave with you. Choose to die empty.

1

Die Empty

Alas for those that never sing,
But die with all their music in them.

—OLIVER WENDELL HOLMES, *THE VOICELESS*

In February 2011, the artist, designer, and urban planner Candy Chang transformed an abandoned home in her New Orleans neighborhood into a living work of art. She had recently lost someone she cared for deeply, and was reflecting on the meaning of life and what truly mattered to her. She was curious to know if other people had similar thoughts about living with a sense of urgency and purpose so she created an enormous chalkboard running the height and width of one side of the abandoned home. She then stenciled the words "Before I Die . . ." at the top of the wall, and created dozens of spaces with the words "Before I die, I want to _____" in grids across the surface. Chang provided the chalk needed to fill in the blanks, and waited in anticipation to see what would happen. Would people participate? Would it be vandalized? Would anyone even notice?

She didn't have to wonder for long. The installation was an immediate hit, as neighborhood residents and passersby filled it with their hopes, dreams, and aspirations. Some of the contributions were impersonal and matter of fact, and some were deeply personal:

"Before I die I want to . . . sing for millions."

"Before I die I want to . . . write a book."

"Before I die I want to . . . understand."

"Before I die I want to . . . tell my mother I love her."

"Before I die I want to . . . be someone's cavalry."

Word quickly spread, and visitors began showing up from throughout the region to inscribe their dreams and creative aspirations on the wall. It wasn't long before others were inquiring about creating installations in their own communities. At present, there have been more than one hundred "Before I die . . ." installations in cities across the globe, and Chang and her collaborators have developed a tool kit and detailed instructions for spreading the movement.

Why did Chang's project take off quickly and become so widely covered by international media? I believe it's because the "Before I Die . . ." wall resonates with what we both know and fear to be true: we have only a certain amount of time available to us, and how we choose to spend our days is significant. We're also aware that there are things we would like to do and experiences we would like to have before we die, many of which are desires we've suppressed for months or even years. We feel the ticking of the clock, and the accompanying sense that we may be missing our opportunity to make a contribution to the world. However, we often ignore these impulses as a result of the relentless pragmatics of life and work.

Your days are finite. One day, they will run out. As a friend of mine likes to say, "You know, the death rate *is* hovering right around one hundred percent." Many people I know spend their entire life trying to avoid this fact. They fill their lives with frantic activity, bouncing from task to task, and no matter how successfully they perform in their work, as they close up shop for the day they are left with the question "Did the work I did today really matter?" Others I've met are incredibly successful at, vested in, and highly compensated for their work, but over time they've grown stagnant. They sense they have something more to give, but they can't quite put their finger on why they're stuck in first gear. They have a nagging suspicion that they are capable of contributing more—maybe even being truly brilliant at *something*—but have no road map for unlocking what that contribution might be.

This begs the obvious question: How do you set in motion a course of action that will allow you to unleash your best, most valuable work while you still can? The marketplace is filled with (often simplistic and unhelpful) platitudes about living a life of fulfillment, landing your dream job, and discovering your purpose, but when you are in the midst of the fray it can feel futile to think about anything other than hitting your deadlines and chasing the next promotion. It's easy to get lost, and wake up many years later in a strange land asking yourself, "Who am I, how did I get here, and how do I go back?"

The only way to avoid this scenario is to instill consistent practices into your life that keep you on a true and steady course. An ounce of preventative discipline today is worth a pound of corrective action later. This book is about cultivating the mind-set and the methods you need to unleash your best work each day, and to increase the odds that, at the end of your life, you will not regret how you spent your days.

Don't Die Full of Your Best Work

In my first book, *The Accidental Creative*, I recounted a meeting in which a friend asked a strange and unexpected question: "What do you think is the most valuable land in the world?"

Several people threw out guesses, such as Manhattan, the oil fields of the Middle East, and the gold mines of South Africa, before our friend indicated that we were way off track. He paused for a moment, and said, "You're all wrong. The most valuable land in the world is the graveyard. In the graveyard are buried all of the unwritten novels, never-launched businesses, unreconciled relationships, and all of the other things that people thought, 'I'll get around to that tomorrow.' One day, however, their tomorrows ran out."

That day I went back to my office and I wrote down two words in my notebook and on the wall of my office that have been my primary operating ethic for the last several years: Die Empty. I want to know that if I lay my head down tonight and don't wake up tomorrow, I have emptied myself of whatever creativity is lingering inside, with minimal regrets about how I spent my focus, time, and energy. This doesn't happen by accident; it takes intentional and sustained effort. But I can say with confidence from my own experience and the experiences of others I've worked with that the effort is well worth it.

You've probably heard "No one ever lay on their deathbed wishing for another day of work." I think this saying is wrong, and perhaps a little dangerous because of what it implies. First, I believe a great many people do regret not having treated their life with more purpose, and would give anything to have one more chance to approach it with the kind of intention and conviction that imminent death makes palpable. They know that they consistently ignored small twinges of intuition, inspiration, and insight. They recall how they cowered away from risk in favor of comfort. They spent their days regretting their past decisions rather than taking aggressive steps to redirect their life in a more hopeful direction.

Second, this saying presupposes that work is an inherently miserable act that people engage in against their will, or that it's something that necessarily pulls us away from the people and activities we really care about. But work encompasses much more than just how we make a living. Any value we create that requires us to spend our time, focus, and energy—whether in the context of occupation, relationships, or parenting—is *work*. Humans, it seems, are wired to find satisfaction by adding value through toil. Thus, for centuries work has been a deeply ingrained part of our identity and our understanding of our place in the world. I believe that the more you apply self-knowledge to how you engage your labor, the more satisfaction you will find in the very act of work, and thus the more joy you will find in life.

If there is one overriding goal of this book it is this: to bring a newfound clarity and sense of urgency to how you approach your work on a daily basis, and over your lifetime. I hope to help you lock onto a focused understanding of what's really important and help you make a commitment to chase after it with gusto rather than simply settling in for the ride.

A Confession

I've struggled to write this book, and in full disclosure, I realize I've got some things working against me. Here's the honest truth: no one really wants to think about death, let alone adopt it as some kind of motivational slogan. In fact, my colleagues and I often laugh as we imagine the words "Die Empty" inscribed on a giant banner behind me as I take the stage at a conference. It's not exactly the kind of feel-good, warm and fuzzy sentiment that large public gatherings are typically designed to cultivate. It would be much safer (and perhaps more lucrative) for me to stay squarely in my lane and continue to write about innovation or collaboration.

And still, I can't *not* write this book. As I've shared this message with thousands of people over the past few years, I've received countless e-mails from around the world about how it's changed their life perspective and challenged them to approach their work with more urgency. At the same time, I continue to encounter professionals every day who are abandoning their contribution and forfeiting their best work because they're stuck or deceived into believing that the path they are on will eventually become more bearable. It pains me to think about their unfulfilled potential while knowing that implementing a few simple, daily practices to eliminate areas of ineffectiveness could set them on the right path. Thus, in writing this book I'm taking my own advice to not leave inside me the work I care about the most.

What Die Empty *Doesn't* Mean

The phrase "die empty" could easily be misunderstood to mean spending every ounce of yourself on your career. I can imagine a sinister, evil-mustached boss manipulating employees with a motivational poster containing the words "DIE EMPTY!" in an attempt to squeeze a little more effort out of the team. This, friends, could not be further from what I hope this book will accomplish.

It's not about getting everything done today

Karōshi is a Japanese term that means "death from overwork." In the past several decades, it has become more common in Japanese culture, which in the years since World War II has heavily emphasized the importance of work productivity over all other aspects of life. Many high-ranking executives have died in the prime of life for no apparent reason other than the ill effects of overwork. To be clear, this is not what I mean by "die empty." It's not about ignoring all areas of your life so that you can exclusively focus on getting work done. In fact, working frantically is actually counterproductive in many cases. Emptying yourself of your best work isn't just about checking off tasks on your to-do list; it's about making steady, critical progress each day on the projects that matter, in all areas of life. Embracing work with this mind-set will not only increase your chances of tackling your goals, but will also make it all more gratifying.

It's not the same as "live like there's no tomorrow"

Opportunity is always accompanied by its twin sibling: responsibility. Today you have a chance to make a difference through your work, but you must also be mindful of how today's actions will affect tomorrow's outcomes, and how your work impacts the lives of others. You must be conscious of how today's choices beget tomorrow's regrets.

It's not about following your whims

You have a responsibility to leverage your passions, skills, and experiences to make a contribution to the world. You also need to make sure that you are delivering on your expectations and honoring the people who are paying you to produce results. The most frustrating part of work for many people is the tug-of-war between making a contribution you believe in and honoring the expectations of your manager or client, even if it means doing work you are less proud of. But as you'll see throughout the book, the tension between these two forces can often be remedied with a subtle shift in mind-set, which will also lead to more satisfaction, and, ultimately, better work.

What Die Empty *Does* Mean

Throughout the rest of this book we will be operating by a set of core beliefs that underlie the practices and principles you'll learn along the way. These beliefs will help you be more purposeful in how you approach your work.

Your days are numbered—finite—someday they will run out

This is indisputable. We live with the stubborn illusion that we will always have tomorrow to do today's work. It's a lie. We need to live with a sense of urgency about the work we do today. It matters not just because an opportunity lost today is an opportunity lost forever, but because the way that we engage in our work ultimately affects the way that we engage in our life as a whole. As you grow in your capacity to engage in your work, and as you discipline yourself to make continuous growth a part of your daily approach, you will find that latent capacities arise in every area of your life. Don't waste the opportunity.

You have a unique contribution to make to the world

This is not self-help mumbo jumbo; it's the truth. It's easier to dismiss this notion than to own up to it and do something about it. You possess a one-of-a-kind combination of passions, skills, and experiences; there is something you bring to your work that no one else could. If you relinquish that power, then it will never see the light of day and you will always wonder "what if?" The price of regret is incalculable.

No one else can make your contribution for you

Waiting for permission to act is the easy way out. Everyone has to play the hand they're dealt. This means that you can't make a habit of pointing fingers, blaming others, or complaining. As painful as it can be, unfairness is baked into every aspect of life, and to make a contribution and empty yourself of your potential, you have to come to terms with it and refuse to be a victim.

Your contribution is not about you

You cannot function solely out of a desire to be recognized for what you do. You *may* be rewarded with accolades and riches for your work. You may also labor in obscurity doing brilliant work your entire life. More likely, you'll fall somewhere in the middle. There is an overemphasis on celebrity and recognition in our culture, and it will eventually be the death of us. Cultivating a love of the process is the key to making a lasting contribution.

Avoid comfort—it is dangerous

If making a significant impact was easy, it would be commonplace. It's not common because there are many forces that lead to stagnancy and mediocrity. For example, some people, whether co-workers, managers, or even friends, may not want you to fully engage in the pursuit of great work because it places an onus on them to do the same. If you begin to rise above the pack, they will quickly try to bring you back to earth. Also, organizations often make it easy to settle in, providing you with a good salary, a nice title, or a sense of stability—the proverbial "golden handcuffs." It's easy to fall in love with these comfortable perks, but the love of comfort is often the enemy of greatness. There's nothing wrong with experiencing comfort as a by-product of your labor, but you can't make it your chief goal. Greatness emerges when you consistently choose to do what's right, even when it's uncomfortable.

Take a stand—don't shape-shift

You are better positioned to make a contribution if you align your work around your values. Don't be a mirror, passively reflecting the priorities of others. You must dig through the rubble to the core principles that guide your life, come hell or high water. Then commit to engaging your work with a clean conscience, knowing that you are holding true to those principles. There is plenty of room to experiment and try new things, but if you don't stand for what you believe in, you will eventually lose yourself in your work.

Your understanding of your "sweet spot" develops over time like film in a darkroom

In baseball, there is a place on the bat called the "sweet spot," the best part with which to strike the ball. It will send the ball soaring a lot farther than if you hit it even a few fractions of an inch off the mark with the same effort. Similarly, you have a "sweet spot" in your life by which you will add the most unique value through your efforts.

Too many people want to come out of the gate with a clear understanding of their life's mission. There is no *one* thing that you are wired to do, and there are many ways you can add value to the world, while operating in your sweet spot. However, these opportunities will only become clear over time as you act. They will develop slowly like film in a darkroom, giving you clues as you experiment, fail, and succeed. You have to try different things, and devote yourself to developing your skills and intuition, before you will begin to see noticeable patterns and understand your unique value. Patience is required. This is a long-arc game, but it must begin now.

You must plant seeds today for a harvest later

What you plant today you reap tomorrow, or further down the road. You must structure your life around daily progress based on what matters to you, building practices and activities that allow you to plant new seeds each day, with the knowledge that you will eventually see the fruits of your labor.

While the universal principles outlined above are not overtly expressed in the remainder of the book, you will find that they inform many of the specific practices you will learn. In the end, my hope is that you will embrace the importance of *now*, and refuse to allow the lull of comfort, fear, familiarity, and ego to prevent you from taking action on your ambitions.

How to Read This Book

Die Empty is divided into three sections. The first three chapters discuss the nature of contribution, why work matters, and why so many brilliant, skilled people end up settling for less than they're capable of. Chapters 4 through 10 share specific principles that will help you cultivate the mind-set and methods to unleash your best work. The final two chapters offer strategies for applying these principles in your daily life, and using them to uncover a deeper sense of cohesion and purpose.

While the entire book is intended to be practical and immediately implementable, there may be some chapters that resonate more than others. If this is the case for you, I'd recommend spending extra time with these chapters and doing the exercises and questions contained therein before continuing with the rest of the book. Doing this may provide an extra measure of clarity as you consider other, less pressing issues. There are also suggestions for sharing the ideas in this book with people you know and work with. I'd encourage you to do so, as one of the best ways to internalize a concept is to teach it to others.

A final word of caution: the following chapters don't contain quick fixes or shot-in-the-arm tactics designed to make you look on the bright side of life. (Of course, in picking up a book titled *Die Empty* I suspect you probably weren't expecting lollipops and rainbows.) While I believe that a positive outlook is critical to maintaining traction, no one is served by false promises of effortless bliss.

Rather, my goal is to tell it to you as straight as I know how. I believe you're capable of more, and that your best work is still ahead of you. However, all the positive thinking in the world will not amount to anything without decisive action. The rest of us need you to act, because if you don't, you're robbing yourself, your peers, your family, your organization, and the world of a contribution that only you can make.

The cost of inaction is vast. Don't go to your grave with your best work inside you. Choose to die empty.

2

Your Contribution

The average man does not know what to do with his life,
yet wants another one which will last forever.

—ANATOLE FRANCE

> **Principle: Your body of work should reflect**
> **what's important to you.**

How much of your day do you spend doing work that you'll
be proud of later?

In his commencement address to the Stanford University class of 2005, the late Apple co-founder and CEO Steve Jobs
exhorted graduates with this:

"I have looked in the mirror every morning and asked myself: 'If today were the last day of my life, would I want to do what I am about to do today?' And whenever the answer has been 'No' for too many days in a row, I know I need to change something."

He continued, "Remembering that I'll be dead soon is the most important tool I've ever encountered to help me make the big choices in life. Because almost everything—all external expectations, all pride, all fear of embarrassment or failure— these things just fall away in the face of death, leaving only what is truly important. Remembering that you are going to die is the best way I know to avoid the trap of thinking you have something to lose. You are already naked. There is no reason not to follow your heart."

The most common response that I've encountered when sharing these words with others is an immediate "YES!" followed by a numb look of "Now what?" The notion of blazing a path into the unknown is exciting, but it can also lead to a kind of "purpose paralysis" (fear of getting it wrong) or worse, frustration when the daily grind of work doesn't seem to reward your pursuit of those flashes of inspiration. It seems like fine advice for someone with no obligations, limitations, or baggage, but not for people living in the real world with grown-up responsibilities such as a family and a mortgage.

However, engaging in deeply gratifying work does not require you to check out of life, pack your bags, and head off on a pilgrimage to India. It simply requires consistent, focused efforts to cultivate your instincts and skills, and make measured progress on your goals. Brilliant work is forged by those who consistently approach their days with urgency and diligence. Urgency means leveraging your finite resources (focus, assets, time, energy) in a meaningful and productive way. Diligence means sharpening your skills and conducting your work in a manner that you won't regret later. When you adopt the mind-set of urgent diligence, you'll pour all of who you are into your days, and subsequently you'll find that the unique value you bring to the world comes more clearly into focus.

Just having a job is, in many cases, a luxury in today's economic climate. The nature of the work and the degree to which it fulfills a desire to engage in something meaningful is of secondary concern for many, and understandably so. You might be asking yourself: Isn't it selfish to think about things like personal fulfillment and being in your "sweet spot" when there are so many people scrambling just to find employment?

Absolutely not! The great problems we see in the world today will not be solved by people functioning at half capacity, cranking out work they don't care about in order to buy more things that will eventually rust or rot. These problems will be solved by people who have tapped into their deeper aptitudes and who are pouring themselves fully into work that's meaningful to them and valuable to others. Unfortunately, despite the often expressed desire to engage in great work, it seems that many people already sense that they are operating at less than their full ability.

A 2012 study sponsored by Adobe and conducted by the research firm StrategyONE interviewed five thousand adults, a thousand each from the United States, the United Kingdom, Germany, France, and Japan, about their perceptions of creativity and creative engagement. The study revealed that while there is an increasing expectation across all sectors for both creativity and productivity, in many workplaces creativity is frequently subverted due to the increasing pressure to get work done. Globally, only one in four people reported that they feel they are living up to their creative potential.

What this sampling reveals is that when we have to choose between doing work we're proud of and just getting the job done, many of us feel compelled to do the latter. We know there's always more work just over the horizon, ready to wash over us like a tsunami. We have to settle for what's practical over pursuing what's possible so that we can live to fight another day. Thus, we save ourselves for tomorrow. But over time, approaching work this way corrodes our sense of purpose and our will to excel. We end up with far too many unexecuted ideas kicking around the back of our minds, and we eventually feel overwhelmed and stuck. We know that we're capable of more.

The truth is there's no deep, dark secret to unleashing your best work and finding your sweet spot. Though not easy, it begins with the decision to build practices that help you scan your life for areas where you might be growing stagnant, and to help you pour more of who you are into your work. Your legacy is built one decision at a time.

Your Body of Work

When you're gone, your work will stand as the single biggest testament to who you were and what you believed. By "your work," I don't just mean your occupation, but any way in which you contribute value to the world using your available resources. This, of course, includes every task you do and project you engage in, but also every time you encourage someone else or contribute to a relationship, every instance in which you make an effort to grow your skills or develop your mind, or every time you go the extra mile even though you are exhausted. Your body of work comprises the sum total of where you choose to place your limited focus, assets, time, and energy. For the purpose of this book, I will define work as any instance where you make an effort to create value where it didn't previously exist.

Naturally, your worth as a person transcends the value you create, but your work is the most visible expression of your priorities. As you consider your current body of work and the sum of the value you've created, is it reflective of what you truly care about? Forget about your title, pay grade, or how the world would rate your relative success or failure compared with what's considered "normal." I've found that the only way to effectively gauge my work is to answer the question *Can I lay my head down tonight satisfied with the work I did today?*

This exact question is posted prominently on my computer monitor, where I see it daily. I wrote it in a moment of frustration about a year and a half ago, when I was at the end of a long season, having just published my first book and wrapped up an extended period of travel. I found myself in a strange land, having just achieved a lifelong goal, but facing the uncertainty on the other side. For so long, my energy had been devoted to the pressures of doing my "regular work" while writing and launching the book in every spare moment, but like a rubber band stretched beyond its elasticity, I simply couldn't return to normal. While I was getting a lot of work done—I still had a business to run, after all—without the singular focus and clarity that the book launch brought, I felt like I was pushing a wall forward but making little meaningful progress. Worse, my family began to feel the effects too. When I was struggling to make meaningful progress at the office, the lack of traction infiltrated my home in the form of a short temper, emotional retreat, and a lack of follow-through on important family matters.

Empty space wants to be filled, and where there is an absence of purposeful activity and meaningful progress, any activity that brings the ping of immediate productivity will fill the void. With a lack of clear purpose to drive your work, efficiency often supplants effectiveness, and it's possible to move ever faster without any sense of direction. "Pointless efficiency" perfectly describes my state during my post-book-launch haze. I was working hard, and getting a lot done, but I felt as though I wasn't really checking the most important items off my list, let alone questioning myself about what *should* be on the list instead of busywork. A bit ironically, it's the same position I'd helped countless others escape, yet here I was slipping on the same patch of ice I'd seen a thousand times.

Even small amounts of success can be the harbinger of complacency—or worse, paralysis—because every milestone you reach ushers in new uncertainty. Where to now? What are the next logical steps? Does this work still matter, or is it time to change course? Because we are biologically hardwired to form habits around rewarding activity, when we accomplish a goal or taste the sweet fruit of success, it's tempting to keep pushing the same levers over and over again. However, this approach is often a fast track to mediocrity. The key to long-term success is a willingness to disrupt your own comfort for the sake of continued growth. To that end, how you choose to stare down uncertainty is often the determinant of success or failure. You can either operate by design, meaning that you put specific measures in place to keep you energized, self-aware, and operating at full capacity, or you operate by default, doing what seems comfortable or easy in the moment until your next steps become more clear. (Hint: they won't.)

In the scenario described above, I was falling prey to one of the most common pitfalls of creative work. In order to feel that I was making progress, I was throwing myself deeply into execution without considering how I was approaching my work, whether I was even headed in the right direction, and if I was using the proper tools. I was leveraging one kind of work but ignoring the other two altogether.

The Three Kinds of Work

Work is core to the human experience. We seem to be wired to derive a sense of purpose from adding the smallest amount of value through our efforts. In his classic book *Working*, in which he gives firsthand accounts of the lifestyles of dozens of workers in diverse occupations, Studs Turkel wrote, "In all instances, there is felt more than a slight ache. In all instances, there dangles the impertinent question: Ought not there be an increment, earned though not yet received, from one's daily work—an acknowledgement of man's *being*?" Work is a reinforcement of that sense of being—of our sense of *belonging*—and a way to discover ourselves as we interact with the world around us.

Even though work sometimes feels like one massive, melded blend of tasks, conversations, and meetings, it can be parsed into three different forms: Mapping, Making, and Meshing. To truly unleash your full capability, and to ultimately find your sweet spot of contribution, you must engage in all three.

Mapping is fairly straightforward. It's planning, plotting your objectives, and setting priorities. It's the "work before the work" that helps you ensure you're spending your focus, time, and energy in the right places. You often map instinctually, as when you make a list of tasks to accomplish, or block off time on the calendar. Sometimes mapping is also done in collaboration with others, such as in strategy meetings or planning sessions.

However, not all the mapping you need to do is instinctual and obvious. It's not all about critical paths and Gantt charts. Some mapping deals with less tangible aspects of work, such as the values that drive you or your sense of why you do what you do. When you fail to account for these in your mapping, it's easy to lose your focus and quickly get off course. You can wind up making really great progress in the wrong direction. In later chapters, you will learn how ignoring these less obvious forms of mapping can cause you to go astray, and some practices you can implement to keep you on your desired course.

Making is actually *doing* the work. It's creating value of any kind, including executing tasks, making sales calls, designing, writing, engaging with your direct reports, and tackling your objectives. Making is what typically comes to mind when you think of work, because it is what you're doing when you deliver the most tangible value. You can strategize all you want, but in the end, you have to do something about your plans. While it's often difficult to measure in the moment how effectively you plan or strategize (Mapping), you *can* count at the end of the day how many tasks you checked off a list, how many words you wrote, or how many calls you made. As a result, it's easy to gravitate toward Making at the expense of the other two kinds of work because you're able to point at something and say "I did that!" As mentioned above, this can result in making quick, but ultimately useless, progress.

Because Making is the most tactical of the three kinds of work, it's also the area where it's easiest to get distracted. There are more moving parts and decisions with immediate impact, and thus there are more opportunities for things to go awry. As such, you must have some guiding principles to help you stay aligned and on task, which we'll discuss in later chapters.

The final kind of work, **Meshing**, is often overlooked because it is rarely tied directly to results. You don't get paid for it, and it doesn't show up on anyone's organizational priority matrix. However, it's often the most important determinant of long-term success and getting the best work out of yourself and your team. Meshing involves all of the "work between the work" that actually makes you effective. It's composed of activities that stretch and grow you, such as acquiring and developing new skills, reinforcing or enhancing your knowledge, cultivating your curiosity, or generating a better understanding of the context for your work. It's also composed of critical disciplines such as paying attention to the adjacent spaces in your industry and engaging in activities that may not have an immediate payoff, but position you to be more effective in the coming days.

In the hustle of daily life, it's easy to overlook Meshing and focus mostly on Mapping and Making, largely because they provide a more immediate payoff. However, you ignore Meshing at your peril, because your diligence about engaging in behavior that has a longer-arc payoff often correlates directly with your long-term success. Continued, disciplined growth prevents stasis.

You need to be purposeful about engaging in all three types of work. This won't happen by default, only by design. All of us have a tendency to gravitate toward one of the three kinds of work at the expense of the others, and while the negative effects of neglect may not be evident in the short term, they can be disastrous in the long term. For example, some people love to plan, but have a difficult time mustering the will to actually do the work. Others love to dive into the work, but fail to regularly step back to define the context and objectives in a way that keeps them on course. Still others are great at planning and executing, but they aren't taking time to expand their knowledge and skills and thus become less effective over time. Depending on how disciplined you are about engaging in the three types of work, there are four profiles you can fall into: Developer, Driver, Drifter, Dreamer.

Mapping + Making + Meshing = Developer

The Developer is constantly weaving together available resources and opportunities to create value. He doesn't work frantically, but instead works with urgency and diligence, making plans and then executing them, learning from his actions, and then redirecting as needed. He recognizes that uncertainty is not an enemy, but a natural part of engaging in important and valuable work. He also knows that opportunities are valuable only if he is prepared to take advantage of them, and as such he is constantly developing the skills that will be needed when he gets where he wants to go rather than where he is currently. If you want to die empty of regret, with a body of work you can be proud of, you must focus on becoming a Developer.

Mapping + Making − Meshing = Driver

The Driver is extremely focused on results, and spends most of his time planning and checking tasks off lists. He is obsessed with today's results, but does little to increase his platform for future effectiveness. As a result, he becomes narrowly effective and is often unable to spot or take advantage of opportunities if they are outside his immediate area of focus.

Someone with a tendency toward being a Driver may begin his career strongly because sheer discipline and the ability to plan and execute separates him from the pack. However, he may slowly wane in performance over time because he is only doing more of the same, but neglecting to grow his skills and develop the intangibles that will allow him to tackle new challenges. Sadly, sheer will and determination is only one element of success. Because of this, the Driver typically fails to unleash his full potential or find his sweet spot.

Making + Meshing − Mapping = Drifter

The Drifter greatly enjoys the process of Making, and loves to develop his skills and engage his curiosity (Meshing), but is a poor planner (Mapping). As a result, he frequently bounces from project to project and goes wherever his latest whim carries him. He has a good work ethic and may even be quite successful in short bursts, but his lack of strategic Mapping means that there is a lot of wasted opportunity and little strategic progress. He lacks the conviction of a long-term plan.

Because of his failure to map effectively, the Drifter fails to follow through on many of his ideas and projects. He gets stuck and doesn't see things through to the end. He may have spotty success, but wonder why his work never seems to sustain itself.

Meshing + Mapping − Making = Dreamer

The final combination is the Dreamer. He is obsessed with ideas and personal growth (Meshing) and strategic plans (Mapping), but lacks the conviction, courage, or work ethic to put his plans in motion (Making). The Dreamer is a talker, but he rarely accomplishes much. He can be effective when he wants to, but quickly loses interest and rarely finishes much of what he starts because he's always moving on to the next great thing.

Every person—and organization—will gravitate toward one profile or another from time to time. (I tend toward the Drifter.) There is nothing inherently wrong with any of the types in moderation, as long as you are aware of how they have the potential to consume your work. To truly put yourself in the best possible position to unleash your best work, you must adopt a Developer mind-set, meaning that you are disciplined about Mapping, Making, and Meshing so that you leverage all the opportunities and resources at your disposal.

Chapters 4 through 10 will address the most common ways people neglect the three kinds of work, and offer tangible practices to help you purposefully engage in them so that you aren't leaving important considerations to chance. As mentioned earlier, most of us are well versed in how to plan a project, and how to organize our days in order to make progress on it. But there are subtle ways in which we can lose our bearing or succumb to stasis if we do not purposefully weed out distractions, or continually ask ourselves if we are still on the right course.

Cultivating the Developer mind-set (Mapping + Making + Meshing) takes time and persistent focus, and a willingness to constantly disrupt and question not only what you're doing, but *how* you're doing it. As you engage with the mind-set of a Developer, actively engaging in all three kinds of work, you will be better positioned to identify the areas where you contribute the most value, the elements of work that are most personally gratifying, and new opportunities that you'd like to pursue. In other words, you will be better positioned to build a body of work that you will be proud of later.

Invisible Impact

In the early 1970s, a Detroit-based singer-songwriter named Rodriguez emerged onto the music scene. He was spotted by music executives while playing a gig in an obscure bar in a run-down part of town, and was quickly put to work recording his first album. The executives were certain that he was destined to be the next Bob Dylan, and that his music was so transcendent it would garner an immediate audience and launch him into international superstardom. Unfortunately, despite some critical acclaim, his debut album sold few copies, and his follow-up album did worse. Despite all the hype, it seemed that Rodriguez was destined for obscurity.

A few years later, as the story goes, a woman visited South Africa to see her boyfriend and happened to bring along a Rodriguez record. Her boyfriend loved the record, and made a copy to share with friends. Copies passed from peer to peer, the buzz built, and Rodriguez rapidly became a cult icon among the youth of apartheid-burdened South Africa. As one man put it, "He was the soundtrack of our lives." His music was as pervasive in the average liberal South African home as that of the Beatles and Simon and Garfunkel. As his fame grew, so did his album sales. Unfortunately for Rodriguez, his record label had folded shortly before this surge of international recognition (he was also big in Australia), and he was completely unaware that he was gaining an audience for his music halfway around the world. Additionally, a legend had emerged in South Africa, which was information starved due to the isolationist regime, that Rodriguez had committed suicide onstage during a concert many years prior. Because of this story, no one bothered to seek him out to see if he was still making music.

While his fame grew half a world away, Rodriguez had returned to working for a demolition company. He lived in a modest home in downtown Detroit, returned to school to get a degree in philosophy, and lived an unassuming existence. That all changed in the early 1990s, when a South African music journalist, Stephen Segerman, was charged with helping write the liner notes for the first release of a Rodriguez CD. Segerman decided to investigate further to see if he could verify some of the legends about his musical hero. He made several phone calls to the United States, and after much persistence was able to contact some of the people involved with the original Rodriguez album projects. To his surprise and bewilderment, Segerman learned that Rodriguez was not only still alive, but that he had not made any new music in decades since his first few albums had supposedly been a commercial disaster. Segerman and his investigative partner Craig Bartholomew created a website dedicated to finding Rodriguez, and eventually uncovered his whereabouts when Rodriguez's daughter responded to one of their inquiries. They chatted with Rodriguez by phone, and invited him to South Africa to perform a series of concerts for his fans.

When they arrived in South Africa in March of 1998, Rodriguez and his daughters expected to be greeted by a few dozen fans excited to hear his music. Instead, his first concert could barely contain the enthusiasm of over five thousand people who packed the venue, singing along with every word of his decades-old songs. The initial concert was followed by several more sold-out shows, each at the same level of intensity as the first. In total, Rodriguez performed for tens of thousands of adoring fans in South Africa before returning to the United States and resuming his life as a demolition worker. His legend and career have since grown, and a 2012 film titled *Searching for Sugar Man* documented the surreal quest to find Rodriguez, and subsequently won the Academy Award for Best Documentary Feature.

Rodriguez spent well over two decades of his life believing that his music had been a commercial failure. He moved on, often working tough jobs in grueling conditions, but always with a mind-set of craftsmanship and artistry. (In the film, his former foreman describes how Rodriguez would arrive at the job site wearing a fancy suit, as if he were headed to a job at a bank, to do work that many people would find demeaning.) Yet half a world away, his music was becoming the soundtrack of a generation of young South Africans.

You don't always know the full impact of your work. In fact, you may not even get to experience the full effect of your work in your lifetime. For every story like that of Rodriguez, there are countless others where the tireless, diligent work of an individual is not recognized. It's highly unlikely that you will ever be pulled onstage in front of thousands of adoring fans.

But consider this: What if this recognition had never been received by Rodriguez? Would that have in any way diminished the quality of his work or its impact?

You are building a body of work today through both *what* you do and *how* you do it. Whether or not your body of work is recognized for its true value is beyond your control. Regardless, the contribution you make will be accomplished through the use of all three kinds of work (Making, Mapping, Meshing). The degree to which your contribution reflects your true potential will be largely determined by how disciplined you are about improving your self-awareness and skills every day.

Beware of stumbling blocks that stand in the way of contribution. There are sticking points that even the most gifted and disciplined person can fall prey to. In the next chapter, we'll address why mediocrity is so seductive and why so many people unwittingly choose it over a life of dedication to excellence.

3

The Siren Song of Mediocrity

*Only those who will risk going too far can possibly
find out how far one can go.*

—T. S. ELIOT

> **Principle: Mediocrity doesn't just happen suddenly; it develops slowly over time.**

E very brilliant achievement begins with a hunch. It's a deep, ineffable knowledge that something great could happen, could be brought into existence, could change the status quo. It doesn't matter if it's the synthesis of string theory or a flawless and innovative execution of this quarter's marketing strategy; all innovations begin as a subtle and intuitive flash in the nether regions of your mind. Perhaps, if you're aware enough to notice it, this insight takes hold and yields useful energy and enthusiasm as you imagine its potential. You entertain it for a while, considering its implications and thinking through how you might make it happen. But your enthusiasm quickly wanes as other forces begin to take hold of you. These are the forces that contribute to stagnancy and self-preservation. They cause you to second-guess your intuition, become obsessed with the reasons the idea would be too difficult to act upon, and inevitably compromise. Over time, that initial, promising hunch fades into the mist, sometimes replaced by a new one, but often lingering like a splinter in your mind that you can't quite shake.

Why does this happen? Why are so many discarded ideas, projects, and opportunities tossed to the roadside, replaced by something easier, safer, and more imminent? Why do so many people start strongly and with such hope, but succumb over time to the siren song of mediocrity?

When we start our career or an exciting project, everything is new. We throw ourselves into the work with full vigor, because we know that we need to prove our worth to our manager or clients. In some ways, it's like a new dating relationship. We put our best foot forward because we want to win the respect and approval of our potential partner. However, over time familiarity sets in and some of the aspects that once seemed new and exciting become predictable and mundane. The tasks we perform no longer stretch us, and some of them we can even do on autopilot. We've lost the thrill of the challenge.

This dynamic is not only present early in our career. It's a cycle that we will go through many times as we take a new job, assume new responsibilities, and settle in for the ride. In each of these situations, we at first feel stretched by the new tasks in front of us, but we gradually adapt to expectations and develop the capacity to deal with them. This growth cycle is rapid and steep early in our career, when we are constantly facing unfamiliar challenges and in need of developing new skills to deal with them. However, as we progress in our career and accumulate more knowledge, there are fewer experiences that instinctively spark our curiosity and challenge us to rise to the occasion. We quickly grow stagnant, relying on our existing skills to perform our work. These skills may be sufficient, and, depending on how innately talented we are, may even earn us a great amount of respect in our industry, but deep down we know that we're not doing our best work. We know that we're coasting. We've succumbed to mediocrity.

The Downside of Success

I met Julie at a workshop I led for her design firm. In her late thirties, Julie is near the top of her industry, and by all accounts has nothing but a great future in front of her. In fact, most people in her field would give anything to have her opportunities and connections. She pulled me aside after the workshop and said that many of the dynamics that I'd taught were things she'd been feeling for a while, but couldn't quite put a name to. She said that as she continues to be rewarded with promotions and new responsibilities, as well as industry-wide recognition, she's had a sinking feeling that she's been slipping into a kind of stasis for quite a while. "I can't put my finger on it, but nothing feels right. I'm still doing my work, but I don't get the same level of satisfaction I once did. I'm making progress, but I don't feel like I'm making *important* progress."

Julie is not alone. I've had similar conversations with many remarkably gifted professionals. They know there's more inside them and they aspire to produce their best work, but it's like there's an invisible force holding them at bay and they feel trapped.

Most of us begin our adult life full of hopes, aspirations, dreams, and enough energy to tackle the challenges we face. We aspire to do great work, to make a mark on the world, and (hopefully) to find work that provides a sense of meaning and purpose. But then—as John Lennon noted—life happens while you're busy making other plans. With new opportunities comes more responsibility, including wonderful things like family, promotions, and more choices about your next steps. However, with more at stake, you can also begin to experience a fear of choosing poorly. The clarity you once experienced has become muddied by options, and you may start to hedge your bets, or make trade-offs in the interest of safety. In the most extreme form, you can become paralyzed with inaction. You may exchange your aspirations for more practical ones, or ones that fit better with the expectations of others.

A term championed in the 1950s by the professor, author, and researcher Herbert A. Simon captures the essence of this phenomenon: *satisficing*. It's the combination of the words "satisfy" and "sufficing," and means selecting an option that is sufficient to meet enough of our ongoing expectations. Simon explained that when dealing with limited resources and an environment of uncertainty, satisficing is sometimes a reasonable approach because our limited resources prohibit us from pursuing every possibility. Therefore, we settle for the best available option that meets most of our requirements. However, Simon himself warned that this strategy isn't always the best one to employ for personal decisions, because there are too many nonrational factors to be considered, and opportunity is not truly unlimited.

When you satisfice, the work that you secretly aspire to do remains inside you. It clogs up the inner workings of your creative process, and causes you to stagnate. You may even begin to lose your compass and overall sense of motivation.

Maybe this isn't you. Maybe you're charging full steam ahead, and feel great about your situation. You are forging into uncharted waters, and doing the best work of your life. Congratulations! However, I'd still encourage you to consider that most people who end up stuck were also once in your situation, and if you aren't attentive you could fall prey to the very same dynamics as Julie did—doing work that others admire, but that you know deep down isn't your best.

No One Charts a Course for Mediocrity

In 1999, the job-search website Monster.com launched a brilliant ad during the Super Bowl called "When I Grow Up." The ad featured a series of kids sharing their dreams, only with a twist.

"When I grow up, I want to file all day long."

"I want to claw my way up to middle management!"

". . . be replaced on a whim."

"I want to have a brown nose."

"I want to be a 'yes-man'!"

The ad finishes by asking the simple question "What did you

want to be?" The subtext of the question, of course, is that you didn't set out for any of these roles when you were young, so why do you settle for one now?

Some would argue that the world is more complicated than this commercial suggests. After all, kids are completely unaware of things such as mortgages, organizational politics, and recessions. True, but the fact remains that many people who start out with promise end up settling along the way for something less. They may rationalize that it is because of external forces, but the reality is that many of them sold themselves out in small ways over time until they could no longer find a way back.

No one charts a course for mediocrity, yet it's still a destination of choice. It's chosen in small ways over time, and those tiny, seemingly inconsequential decisions accumulate until they result in a state of crisis. By that point, making a change often feels overwhelming.

Please note that mediocrity doesn't mean doing poor work or failing to achieve success in your career. You can appear very successful to others, but know deep down that you're settling. At the same time, you might seem outwardly unimpressive to others yet be maximizing your abilities. Mediocrity is thoroughly subjective and relative.

The key to avoiding this slippery slope isn't just to work harder or longer; it's to ensure that you are intentionally disrupting your own work rather than circling the wagons and protecting the ground you've already taken.

The Slippery Slope

Mediocrity doesn't always mean underperforming—it's a sliding scale and a state of mind. It means settling in and succumbing to stasis. Mediocrity comes from the Latin words *medius*, meaning middle, and *ocris*, meaning rugged mountain. Literally translated, it means to settle halfway to the summit of a difficult mountain. It's a compromise of abilities and potential; a negotiation between the drive to excel and the biological urge to settle for the most comfortable option.

When people begin to experience the lull of mediocrity, they often question whether they are in the right job. They wonder if there might be another one out there that would better suit them, and that might give them the thrill they once experienced before things went south. They may even act on that impulse, hopping to another job or company, and subsequently find that everything is better for a while. The newness is back, and that craved-for sense of challenge has returned. Problem solved? Actually, no. In many of these situations the job hopper is right back in crisis within a matter of months. It's not that there's anything wrong with their new job; it's because they changed their external situation without changing their mindset and methods. They were trying to solve an internal problem by changing their external circumstances, which rarely works. You have to begin by finding alignment internally, then question your work environment.

People who are successful over the long arc, and who continue to produce in new and interesting ways after they are well established in their career, refuse to allow circumstances to define their engagement. They continue to grow, develop new skills, and seek unanticipated opportunities to use their skills to create value.

The waxing and waning of enthusiasm for your work is actually somewhat predictable. There are distinct phases of growth that you pass through as you adapt to a new environment or master any skill. These phases can be plotted along the "learning curve," which is a representation of the difficulty of learning a skill plotted along with the benefits of skill acquisition. For complex adaptation, the learning curve tends to look more like a typical "S curve," with slow growth at first, then rapid growth as the fundamental mechanics of the skill become easier to perform, followed by a slow leveling off. This is because complex skills and environments are nuanced and require a good amount of time to master, but the benefits of mastering them are substantial. (This is why specialists in highly complex fields are typically well compensated.)

Acquiring new skills and adapting to complex, uncertain environments isn't easy, though. It requires persistent attention and near-constant effort to maintain a trajectory of growth. As such, it's easy to grow tired or lose your drive. However, when you stop growing, you start dying. In much the same way that an organization needs to be persistently innovative in order to maintain market share, individuals must make a personal commitment to lifelong personal innovation through skill development, risk-taking, and experimentation in order to avoid stagnation. The seeds of tomorrow's brilliance are planted in the soil of today's activity.

Throughout the remaining chapters of this book we will examine actions that you can take today to unleash the great work inside you in a sustainable way. While there is no predictable formula for growth, there are certain practices and principles that can position you to stay ahead of the challenges you will face, and help you maintain your progress up the rugged mountain you are climbing. This will require you to step back from your work frequently to examine not just what you're doing, but how and why you are doing it. Even if you've heard of some of the practices before, don't allow that to dissuade you from implementing them. It is action that creates impact, not knowledge alone.

Remember, there are three kinds of work that you must be persistently engaged in to be effective: Mapping, Making, and Meshing. In my work with individuals and organizations, I've witnessed several key areas where mediocrity repeatedly creeps in and causes neglect of one of these three kinds of work, leading to ineffectiveness. Because they're such common and destructive slipping points, I call them the "Seven Deadly Sins of Mediocrity." To make them easier to remember, I've also named and organized them alphabetically, "A-B-C-D-E-F-G."

Aimlessness

If you were to put a blindfold on me, then hand me a bow and arrow and ask me to shoot at a target, I would have absolutely no clue where to aim my shot. If I knew the general direction of the target, I might get lucky and hit it once out of a thousand attempts, but there would be no way to replicate the effort because it would be quite literally a "blind shot." Even if I did hit the target accidentally, there would be little joy for me because it would be the result of chance and not due to strategic effort. There is little personal gratification in unintentional success.

This is an illustration of aimlessness. Over time, without a clear strategy or metric for success, I would eventually become weary from trying to hit the target, and would conclude that my actions lacked any kind of meaningful purpose. I may even stop trying altogether, because there is no personal benefit in doing so; a victory isn't gratifying if it's pure luck. Or someone may try to incentivize me to keep me plucking the bow. For example, if they paid me by the shot, I would take as many as possible regardless of their accuracy. I would still be aimless and my work would seem futile, but I would at least have a metric to go by: the more pointless shots I take, the more money I make.

Aimlessness is a destructive force because it removes both the joy of success and the gratification that comes from hard, focused work. In order to be effective and contribute meaningfully, you need to apply points of traction in your life to prevent aimlessness from becoming the norm. You have to define the battles that are important to you, and align your resources to fight them.

It's important to note that aimlessness does not mean the lack of a drive to succeed. I've met many focused, talented, driven people who simply lack anything substantive that they could call a central theme for their work. Aimlessness means a general lack of cohesiveness within your day-to-day activities. In other words, you may be doing great work, and you may be doing a lot of work, but you're not making progress in a way that is personally meaningful.

Some people try to counter aimlessness by setting big goals, and steeling their resolve to accomplish them, but this effort can be just as pointless and aimless. Committing to drive to the other side of the country does you no good if you're not certain why you're going there. Similarly, big goals will do you no good unless you have perspective on which conflicts are truly worth your putting it all on the line.

The key to conquering aimlessness is to concretely define the battles that you need to fight each day in order to make meaningful progress, then focus your efforts on those above all else.

Boredom

Have you ever heard the saying "only boring people get bored"? It's wrong. Boredom isn't necessarily a bad thing; it's how we handle boredom that determines whether it becomes a trigger for productivity or stagnancy. Boredom is often a sign that you're poised for a breakthrough in your work. It means your mind has grown weary of the rut you're in and is ready to jump the tracks and try something new. The problem is that rather than trying to use boredom to our advantage, we often succumb to it and allow it to zap our brain of its creative firepower.

The cure for boredom is intentional and applied curiosity. To be successful intellectually and professionally you need to maintain a level of disciplined curiosity, which means staying in touch with your deeper questions, and practicing the mechanics of divergent problem solving.

While some people are more innately curious than others, it's possible to build practices into your life that help you leverage your natural curiosity and channel it into the problems that you encounter each day. Perhaps more important, stoking the fires of your curiosity will help you identify important problems you may have previously overlooked. Problem finding is increasingly more critical than problem solving.

Comfort

In *The Accidental Creative*, I wrote that "the love of comfort is frequently the enemy of greatness" in life and work. When comfort becomes the goal of life, we cannibalize future progress for the sake of temporary stability. This dynamic isn't just limited to individuals. Organizations can easily become too comfortable with existing practices, products, or market presence and cease to innovate. This was the primary issue Clayton Christensen addressed in *The Innovator's Dilemma*. At a certain point, past innovations inhibit future innovations. Once ground has been taken by an organization, it turns its efforts to protecting that ground rather than taking new ground. This means that other companies are able to attack the periphery of the market and weaken the dominant player's position.

The key to overcoming the ill effects of a love of comfort is a commitment to continual growth and skill development. One of the saddest things I see in my work is when an individual achieves a certain level of success in their career and, out of comfort or overconfidence, stops focusing on developing their skills. This inevitably leads to stagnation and decreasing returns on their effort. To avoid this, you must identify relevant skills that will help you continue to contribute, build practices into your life to help you develop them, and have frequent checkpoints through which you gauge your progress and redirect as necessary.

Delusion

A few years ago, the "televised talent show" craze swept the world, flooding millions of our homes on a weekly basis with new aspiring singers, dancers, comedians, and more. Shows such as *American Idol*, *The X Factor*, *America's Got Talent*, and others feature ordinary people stepping onto the stage in hopes of capturing the once-in-a-lifetime chance to launch their career as a performer. Unfortunately, while there are many brilliant performances along the way, these shows also feature many cringe-worthy moments, as some who audition for their shot are obviously just not qualified. Amazingly, the response of many of these candidates when receiving an honest assessment of their skills is something between surprise and utter shock. They often storm offstage, accompanied by their loved ones, crying and declaring that the judges don't know what they're missing. It makes for compelling television, but it's quite sad to see people who have been so obviously deluded by friends and family into believing that they have a talent, when even the most tone-deaf person would agree that they don't.

To add the value you're capable of adding, you need to cultivate self-awareness. You must have an accurate sense of your skills, your weaknesses, and your core drivers. Then, you need to orient your daily activity around that self-knowledge so that you are building on a solid foundation rather than on wishful thinking. Self-delusion is a fast track to a life of wasted potential.

Ego

No matter how successful or skilled you are, you will inevitably fail at many things in your work. For some people, the stigma of failure is simply unbearable. They will do anything to avoid the appearance of failure, including spinning their failures into successes, or denying them altogether. They would rather go down with the ship than admit that the ship might be sinking. Over time, they become inflexible and unwilling to adapt or learn because their ego stands in the way.

To countermand ego, you must adopt a posture of adaptability. This means being in a state of continual learning and openness to correction. Failure is never the ultimate goal; it should be a learning experience rather than a shaming experience.

Fear

When my children were younger, they were afraid of the dark. I tried my best to explain to them that there was nothing in their room once the light went off that wasn't there a split second earlier, but my arguments failed because their fear was irrational. Even though they agreed with my logic, they were certain that the sound of a light switch flicking to "off" opened a portal to the boogeyman's lair. Their fear was rooted in what they *couldn't* see.

Fear thrives on the unknown. Its paralyzing effects are often rooted more in imagination than reality. The key to countermanding fear is to instill a practice of strategic, intentional, and purposeful risk-taking in your life and work. In other words, to experiment, play, and find your voice through taking small chances to express yourself through your work.

Guardedness

Great work happens most consistently in the context of community. Regardless of what kind of work you do, you probably depend on others, whether co-workers, managers, clients, or mentors, in order to accomplish it. But when life is flush with obligations and pressures, the first thing that often gets the boot is our relationships. We may neglect them during busy seasons, or allow tension to build until it's almost unbearable. When this happens, it's easy to go into isolation mode and just keep your head down, cranking away at your work. But when you isolate yourself from other people, you cut yourself off from some of the most valuable opportunities to grow and collaborate.

The solution to guardedness is to build a system of checks into your life to help you scan for relational outages, and to remedy them before they become destructive.

You must be on the lookout for the Seven Deadly Sins of Mediocrity and eliminate them whenever you can. The best defense is almost always an at-the-ready offense.

In a commencement address at Sarah Lawrence College, the author Ann Patchett exhorted graduates that when life doesn't go the way they expect, it doesn't necessarily mean that life has gone wrong. The secret, she said, is "finding the balance between going out to get what you want and being open to the thing that actually winds up coming your way." This is the path of the Developer, and in the following chapters you will learn how to leverage the more ineffable aspects of Mapping, Making, and Meshing to unleash your best work each day.

4

Define Your Battles

The thing that cowardice fears most is decision; for decision always scatters the mists, at least for a moment.

—SØREN KIERKEGAARD

Principle: To counter aimlessness, you must define your battles wisely, and build your life around winning them.

In high school, I developed an obsession with golf. As an introvert, the challenge of the game combined with the long, quiet walks provided the perfect outlet. Like many people, my first attempts to play were profoundly terrible. I was so bad that I often missed the ball multiple times on the same tee. In feat that seemed to defy the laws of physics, I once sent the ball zipping backward (through my own legs), inches from my friend's head, and onto another tee box. It was quite a show. For amusement, my friends would gather around to watch me tee off, while keeping a safe distance, of course.

I determined that I needed to get much better at making contact with the ball if I wanted to improve my score. I spent hours hitting balls on the practice range, driving the ball farther and with more accuracy each week. Over the course of a few years, I actually became quite good. I routinely outdrove my friends, sending the ball soaring dozens of yards past theirs down the middle of the fairway. This only encouraged me to spend more hours on the range, improving the distance of my drive. Now people would gather around the first tee for a different reason: to watch me rocket the ball out of view.

Meanwhile, my friends spent those same hours on the practice green putting and working on their "short game." They became brilliant at hitting long putts and scrambling to rescue their score when they failed to land the ball close to the hole. They couldn't hit the ball nearly as far as I could, but they were consistent, down the middle every time, and, unlike me, they rarely got themselves into trouble on the course.

Here's the thing: my score improved markedly at first, but after a while I plateaued. My friends were soon outscoring me, and chipping strokes off their score with each passing week. My long game was impressive, but I'd forgotten that the point of golf isn't to hit the ball a long distance, it's to put the ball in the hole with as few strokes as possible. There's an old adage in golf that says you "drive for show, putt for dough." You may look impressive off the tee, but a good score is obtained by paying close attention to the "short game," or putting the ball in the hole consistently while under pressure.

I learned something quite valuable from this experience. First, I discovered that while the big, long drives were impressive, and they perhaps saved me some embarrassment, they weren't necessarily going to help me accomplish my true objective: a better golf score. I had—pardon me for this—taken my eye off the ball. The second thing I learned was that progress is often made through one's willingness to persist at the small activities that no one else sees, but that truly generate results. The small battles, when properly defined, eventually lead to victory.

Success in emptying yourself of your best work each day depends on your ability to define the right battles, and do the small but critical tasks that will help you progress toward your true objectives rather than just the ones that others expect you to strive for.

Defining Your Through Line

Have you ever thought about what's truly important to you? What battle would you be willing to fight anytime for any reason? What triggers your primal instinct to act?

Your through line is the theme of your life and work. It's your thesis statement. It's the "delta," or the change, that you wish to see in the world through your efforts. Unfortunately, the complexity of the modern workplace can squelch our sense of mission and cause us to drift. We grow numb to the prompts and cues that once lit a fire inside of us.

Some "calls to arms" that were once vibrant and clear to us can subtly fade over time. Perhaps we are admonished to be ractical, patient, and realistic. Over time, we learn the art of compromise. The problem is we often compromise the most valuable thing: the fire that drives our best work.

You know those cartoons where the devil shows up and offers someone a million dollars in exchange for their soul? In real life, selling out rarely happens that way. It's much more subtle. Sadly, many sell their soul for much less than a million dollars, and over a much longer period of time. They sell out by ignoring their intuition in order to fit in or to make a run for the next promotion, by ignoring potentially risky opportunities in order to go for a sure bet, and by strapping themselves with consumer debt to the point that they're stuck in an endless cycle of working just to pay for things that have already lost their luster.

Most important, people sell their souls by running away from the battles they know they should be fighting. Instead, they become mercenaries. Guns for hire. They don't care which battle they're fighting as long as the checks clear.

Identifying a through line around which to devote your focus, time, and energy is a journey, not a onetime task. The process requires persistence and a good deal of self-awareness, both of which can be challenging to muster when you are already managing the complexity of expectations, objectives, and relationships that comprise an average workday.

In truth, it's perfectly possible to do great work without a cohesive through line, and even to make a substantial contribution. However, having a lens through which to view your efforts and gauge your progress will increase your likelihood of creating a body of work you will be proud of, even if that lens adapts and changes over time.

If you want to lay your head down each night satisfied with

how you spent your day, it's important that you draw the right battle lines, and stand on principle in how you engage your work. You must have a clear understanding of what's important to you, and refuse to compromise in those places that require swift and immediate action. You will eventually come to regret the times when you compromised your contribution for the sake of acceptance by others.

Misguided Passion Can Fuel Aimlessness

Lauren and I met over coffee at a local Starbucks. She contacted me through a colleague to obtain some career advice, as she had recently graduated from college and was trying to figure out what to do next. She was in a fortunate position in that she was able to craft her own degree by mixing together elements of design, business, and social science research methods. This meant that she was able to combine many of her interests into a one-of-a-kind degree, but that unique education was also making it difficult to find a job that matched her highly specialized skill set.

Lauren explained that she had just returned from a conference in which much of the career advice was about taking risks, obliterating fear, and following your passion. There was a lineup of speakers designed to rev up the group and get them excited about conquering the world, but at the end of the event she felt more confused than ever.

"So much of the advice my generation hears is about 'following your passion' and 'trusting your intuition.' Everyone gets very excited when they hear this sort of advice, but in the back of my mind I kept wondering what it all means. What if I mess it up? What if I choose the wrong thing? Am I really devoting my life to something that matters?"

Lauren went on to articulate that one of the biggest fears she and her friends experience is that they won't live up to their full potential.

"We've been told since the time we were very young that we had so much to offer the world. Now that we're setting out on our own, we are concerned that we're going to miss out on the real value we have to offer. We are terrified that we're not going to live up to those expectations and that we'll waste our lives on things that we'll regret later."

The inherent problem with the advice "follow your passion" is that it frames the conversation as if you are the center of the world, or as if a state of joy, bliss, or fulfillment is the objective of life. When this is your mind-set, you're starting off with the wrong question, and will ultimately spend your life chasing after the next buzz when things get dull. The most fulfilled people I've encountered in the marketplace approach their work, in any context, with the question "What can I add?" rather than "What can I get?" They choose worthy battles, then engage in them with everything they have.

The Passion Fallacy

We misuse the word "passion" to describe anything in which we are remotely interested. I might say that I have a passion for playing the guitar, reading, or the TV show *Mad Men*, and then in the next sentence talk about the passion I feel for the work that I do. Thus, when we hear advice like "follow your passion," we equate it to following our whims. We hear quips like "find the right job and you'll never work a day in your life" and we think that there is a panacea awaiting us if we can only tap into our *real* passion. This misunderstanding has led to confusion about where valuable contributions come from and has created a false notion of what it means to engage in gratifying work.

"Passion" has its roots in the Latin word *pati*, which means "to suffer or endure." Therefore, at the root of passion is *suffering*. This is a far cry from the way we casually toss around the word in our day-to-day conversations. Instead of asking "What would bring me enjoyment?" which is how many people think about following their passion, we should instead ask "What work am I willing to suffer for today?"

Great work requires suffering for something beyond yourself. It's created when you bend your life around a mission and spend yourself on something you deem worthy of your best effort. What is your worthwhile cause?

All Passion Is Not Equal

What you want to identify is *productive* passion, the sort of passion that motivates you and is also beneficial to others. Productive passion is others-focused, not self-focused. It is what drives you to labor "on behalf of" rather than to simply satisfy your own needs, though it may stoke your own fires as well. It's what drives you to work a little later than necessary, or to exhibit an extra measure of craftsmanship. Here are a few contributing sources of productive passion:

Compassionate Anger

What fires you up, gets your blood boiling, or otherwise creates in you an urgency to act? Note the very important distinction of *compassionate* anger. This isn't the same thing as road rage, frustration with poor customer service, or feeling irked when you're disrespected. The word "compassion" means to "suffer with." Where do you see dynamics in the marketplace or the world at large that cause you to feel a desire to step in on behalf of those who are suffering in order to bear part of their burden or rectify a wrong?

Though it certainly can be the case, this doesn't have to mean that you're working to overcome some pressing social ill. Your compassionate anger may be on behalf of an underserved market or a group of people who are not being given an adequate platform or the tools they need to do their work. In either case, you are making a conscious decision to step into their battle and suffer with them. It is *com-passion*. (For example, my personal mission is driven primarily by the compassionate anger I feel on behalf of overworked, undervalued creative professionals.)

What do you see, hear, read, or experience that fills you with compassionate anger? Can that knowledge help you choose the battles you should be fighting?

Obsession

If you survey history, you'll find many people who engaged in missions that they probably would have preferred to avoid altogether, but they were swept up and became obsessed with solving a problem they were uniquely equipped to tackle. They may have even been reluctant to engage, but they resolved to act. Over time, this obsession with the problem translated to passion, or a willingness to suffer on behalf of their work. In other words, passion followed action, not the other way around. Think about this in a grand and historical context (the American Founding Fathers who spent months and years away from their families and businesses in order to represent the interests of their fellow oppressed citizens); the business context (Bill Gates and Paul Allen spending weeks obsessing over code in order to produce the product that would become the foundation of Microsoft); and the social context (Scott Harrison, founder of Charity Water, who left his life as a nightclub promoter to solve problems he saw among the poor and underresourced people of West Africa). None of these people seemed (by their own reports) to be driven by the idea that their work would be fun and fulfilling—the standard way we think about passion—but they were willing to address certain problems, even at great personal cost.

As you survey your life, are there specific problems that you find yourself consistently gravitating toward? Are there issues that drive others to come to you for help, and that you seem uniquely equipped to handle, even if it's at personal cost to you?

Hope and Aspiration

Where do you consistently see possibilities that others overlook? Where are you helplessly optimistic even in the face of overwhelming odds, to the point that you will continue to work long after others have given up?

Curtis Martin was inducted into the 2012 class of Football League Hall of Fame. Martin spent te NFL, and finished his career fourth in all-time rus

be

all metrics, he was one of the most successful running backs in history, but he surprised the audience at his Hall of Fame induction when he began his formal remarks with "You know that I was never a football fan. I wasn't the type of guy to watch football. I could probably count on one hand how many football games I've watched from beginning to end in my lifetime."

In his speech, Martin said that football had merely been a last refuge for him as a troubled teen from a broken family. He didn't even play football until his senior year in high school. Further, he confessed, "I'm up here because of how many yards I ran. Everyone who knows me also knows that I hate to run. I don't like to run at all. I box now to stay in shape just because I don't want to run anywhere."

How can one of the greatest running backs of all time— someone with an envied dedication to excellence in his field and the drive to be the best at his role—be ambivalent toward the game in which he excelled? It turns out there's more to the story.

When he recounted the fateful phone call from the legendary NFL coach Bill Parcells indicating that he'd been drafted, Martin relayed the story this way: "My family and I were sitting around and were watching the draft. The phone rings and it's Bill Parcells. I answer the phone and say 'Hello,' and Parcells says, 'Curtis, we want to know if you're interested in being a New England Patriot.' I said, 'Yes, yes, sir.' And we hang up the phone. As soon as we hang up the phone I turned around to everyone and I said, 'Oh my gosh, I do not want to play football.'"

Martin said that one of the other people present on draft day was his pastor, Leroy Joseph. Joseph quickly reframed the conversation by reminding Martin of all of the great things he might able to do for other people, such as single mothers and kids who came from broken and abusive homes. He told Martin that the platform an NFL career would grant him might be a wonderful opportunity to do everything he'd always said he'd like to do.

"That became my connection with football," Martin continued in his speech. "I don't know if he wouldn't have said that to me if football would have gotten out of me what it got out of me. I definitely wouldn't be standing here. And ever since he said that, I knew the only way I was going to be successful at this game called football is if I played for a purpose that was bigger than the game itself, because I knew that the love for the game just wasn't in my heart."

Martin had defined his battle by tapping into a deeper cause—one that transcended his own interests and desires—in order to make a valuable contribution in his chosen field. His clear sense of mission drove him to excel on the football field and off. In his rookie season with the Patriots, he began committing a minimum of 12 percent of every paycheck to his newly formed Job Foundation, which he formed to help single mothers and disadvantaged youth. (He now commits a minimum of 20 percent of his income to the foundation.) Football was a means to an end, and even though Martin's playing days are over, his mission continues.

What are you aspiring toward, on behalf of others? What hope do you have for creating change, and how can you work in order to bring it about?

Welcome to the Battle

No army would charge into battle without battlefront. It would be mass suicide. Yet, daily with our work. While most people h the tasks and projects they're accountable for, they haven't taken the time to consider what they really care about, and how it will find form in their work. They are lost in the fog of war.

Priorities are difficult. When you choose one thing to focus on, you automatically choose not to focus on others. This is why some people fall into aimlessness: they don't like the discomfort of having to say no to very good things that aren't the *most* important things. They'd rather be mediocre at a lot of things than take a real swing at things they care about and risk failure.

The rest of this chapter features questions to help you establish your battle lines. Remember, you cannot fight on every front. You must choose your battles wisely, and win them every time. Small victories will increase your level of confidence and mastery, but consistent failure due to setting the bar too high will lead to frustration and continued aimlessness.

What will you stand for today? What will you refuse to compromise on, no matter what? What will define your terms of engagement?

One of my favorite mission statements is from the Boca Restaurant Group: "Blow People Away." It gives everyone from chefs to managers to servers an actionable operating code by which to approach their work. There are many stories of servers going to extreme efforts to amaze and overwhelm customers, and every time one of these stories circulates it becomes a testament to the company's mission, both internally and externally. It's also a frame for evaluating every customer interaction: "Did I blow them away?" In every interaction, every meeting, every ~~~~ision they make, employees are challenged with the initial-~~~~PA." It's their chosen battle line. What's yours?

What do you know you should be doing, but have been ignoring? These are forgotten battlefronts. They are things that have been weighing on your mind for a while now, and things that you care deeply about, but you've been ignoring because either (a) you fear that you won't have time for them or (b) you haven't defined them enough to know your next steps.

I frequently encounter this issue with entrepreneurs and creative professionals. They have an idea in the back of their mind that they'd like to tackle, and it excites them when they consider it, but they fear that once they take a few steps the project will become overwhelming and they'll fail. One young entrepreneur that I met had been tossing around the idea for a business for quite some time, but he never took even the smallest steps to make it happen. Every time we got together, he'd mention the idea and how great he thought it could be. Finally, after several such instances, I told him, "I don't want you to say another word about that idea. You think it's great, and I think it's great, but it's a figment. It's not real—it's just an idea. Unless you're going to take a step toward making it happen, I don't want to hear about it again." He looked at me with wide eyes. I don't think anyone had spoken to him so honestly before. By all indications, most people just told him how great the idea was, and how it was going to be huge— someday. We agreed that rather than talking about it, he would take one small step each day toward making it happen. Action defines reality, and "potential" is nothing but unproven, hypothetical value.

Make a list of the things you know—deep down—you should be doing, but haven't taken action on. Include as many as you'd like—you don't have to do them all today. (In a minute we'll discuss what we're going to do with the list.)

Where are your "open loops"? These are the unfinished projects, the halfhearted efforts, or the unreconciled relationships. They are the projects that you're afraid to say no to, but deep down you know that you can't commit to. These must be either acted upon and made a priority, or immediately closed and put aside. If you have too many open loops in your life, it diminishes your ability to focus on the mission-critical things. You must become good at pruning your projects and commitments so that you have energy available for your most important work.

Make a list of your open loops, and be as exhaustive as possible.

The key takeaway is this: *To avoid aimlessness, you have to stand for something.* Don't allow aimlessness to rob you of years of your life. You will ultimately be remembered for—and your body of work will be built upon—the battles you chose to spend your time fighting. Act with urgency and diligence today to define your through line and your battles, then carefully allocate your focus, time, and energy on things that matter to you. There are battles that only you are equipped to fight, and while I can't tell you what they are, I suspect you probably already know at least some of them. We need you to act, and we need you to do it now. Run to the battle.

CHECKPOINT

At the end of each of the remaining chapters, you'll be given a set of questions to help you consider how you can apply the principles you've learned. These "checkpoints" will help you stay aligned and focused on your most critical work. They are also designed to help you ensure that the three types of work (Mapping, Making, Meshing) are represented and that you are staying on a course of contribution and growth.

Here are the questions you should ask to help you combat aimlessness and establish battle lines:

What will I stand for today? Look at your calendar and your task list. Think through potential challenges you may face, and how you will deal with them if they arise. What will you refuse to compromise on? What battles will you be required to fight?

What one action will I take today on a forgotten battlefront? Look at your list of things you need to be acting on, and choose one activity to engage in today that will move the project forward. It doesn't have to be huge, but make sure it's something you value.

What open loop can I close? Examine your list of open loops, and choose one to close today. It could be a conversation you've been avoiding or a project that you need to decline. Open loops will weigh you down and steal energy from your more pressing, mission-critical work. Dedicate fifteen to thirty minutes today to act on an open loop and make progress in a meaningful way to close it.

Share this principle: Get together with a colleague or friend and discuss the questions that will help you define what work you are willing to suffer for (your passion). They can be found in the earlier sections on compassionate anger, obsession, and hope and aspiration, but are listed below for convenience:

What do you see, hear, read, or experience that fills you with compassionate anger? What does it mean for the battles you should be fighting?

As you survey your life, are there specific problems that you find yourself consistently gravitating toward? Are there issues that drive others to come to you for help, and that you seem uniquely equipped to handle, even if it's at a personal cost to you?

What are you aspiring toward, on behalf of others? What hope do you have for creating change, and how can you work in order to bring it about?

5

Be Fiercely Curious

Everything has been said before, but since nobody listens we have to keep going back and beginning all over again.

—ANDRÉ GIDE

Principle: To prevent boredom from dulling your senses, you must approach your work with a curious mind-set.

All great feats and brilliant accomplishments, regardless of their nature, begin with a question: Why? How? What if? The response to that question leads to another one, which provokes another, and so on. The pursuit of sustained, great work demands a commitment to pursuing the answers to a never-ending series of inquiries. However, in dealing with the pragmatic elements of daily life and work, our curiosity can become worn and obscured by a tangle of tasks and expectations. We can fall out of touch with our deeper questions and lose the will to ponder.

As a child, curiosity comes naturally. Even though the pursuit of new knowledge is work, it doesn't *feel* like work. The world is a child's laboratory, and everything is mysterious. As our minds begin to consolidate our imaginary and real experience into one cohesive view of the world, our neural networks form patterns of understanding that help us predict what will happen next, mostly so that we can learn to spot opportunity and danger. We see everything unfamiliar within the framework of what we already know, and we discard information that isn't relevant. While these winnowing filters may allow us to process and assimilate new information more efficiently, they also create conceptual boxes that we have to work hard to push out of if we want to reclaim that sense of wonder. We must build disciplines that help us stoke our innate curiosity and allow us to embrace mystery.

This is easier said than done when there are tasks to be checked off and projects to be navigated. In the war between possibilities and pragmatism, the latter wins every time when the pressure is on. But while a curious, questioning mind-set may seem inefficient when we're under pressure to deliver quick results, it actually makes us more effective in everything we do.

The Busily Bored

The phrase I use for highly productive but mentally stagnant professionals is the "busily bored." They're cranking through a lot of work, and they're doing what they have to do to meet their expectations, but if you looked under the hood you'd see that they're bored silly. They no longer find their work stimulating, and they're kind of going through the motions.

They're not stretching their mind.

They're not acknowledging their deeper questions.

They're not trying new things.

They're living with unchecked, limiting assumptions.

The saddest part is that when confronted with a topic other than work, they light up with enthusiasm and delight. If you get them talking about something they're naturally interested in, they'll go on in remarkable detail for several minutes. The problem isn't that they lack the capacity for wonder and interest; it's that they can't seem to apply the same level of curiosity to their work.

The solution to the dilemma? Reclaim curiosity by embracing an *engagement* mind-set rather than an *entertainment* mind-set. This means dedicating yourself to the pursuit of new and better questions, attuning your mind to dive deeply into important problems, and questioning the assumptions that sometimes limit fresh new perspectives.

Entertainment vs. Engagement

Yesterday I stopped in the local coffee shop for an afternoon pick-me-up and to do a little writing. As I stood waiting, I glanced around at the others in the line. Everyone was staring at their cell phone, checking e-mail, texting, or browsing the Web.

I suddenly realized how often those little spaces "in between" are now filled by entertainment. If I am bored for the slightest moment, I can immediately find something to satisfy my need for a fun distraction. When I have nothing to work on (or sometimes even when I do), I can check Twitter, e-mail, or browse my favorite websites for something to entertain me. The never-ending stream of new stimuli is seductive, and I can dip my toe in anytime I feel slightly bored.

However, when I reflect on some of the best ideas I've had in my life and in my work, they often occurred in the spaces "in between" my commitments. They materialized when I least expected, during a moment of downtime, and typically when I was doing something in no way related to the project. Today I don't know if those ideas would even appear on my radar because there are so many distractions pulling at my attention. I often don't notice my environment, overhear fragments of conversation, or notice connections and subtlety the way that I used to, because I've been trained to give my focus to whatever pops up on my screen.

This is the blessing and the curse of technology. It broadens our scope of familiarity with what's happening in the world, but overfamiliarity has undesirable side effects. We may think we understand something, but the depth of our knowledge is more shallow. We often don't take time to stop and consider how what we're seeing or experiencing fits into the wider scheme of our life, because there's always something new to move on to. There is more opportunity for entertainment, but less of the breakthrough synthesis that often comes from deep, purposeful engagement with experiences.

In *The Shallows*, Nicholas Carr reflects on how the human experience is being shaped by emerging technology: "What the Net seems to be doing is chipping away my capacity for concentration and contemplation. Whether I'm online or not, my mind now expects to take in information the way the Net distributes it: in a swiftly moving stream of particles. Once I was a scuba diver in the sea of words. Now I zip along the surface like a guy on a Jet Ski." Carr is implying that many of us ride along the surface of a sea of entertaining content, but rarely engage deeply, consider the implications of what we see, and form patterns of understanding.

The move from depth diver to Jet Skier has significant implications for how we interpret events in our life. While it might seem like this kind of immersive environment would stoke the fires of curiosity, the effect can often be the opposite. We can become numbed by the constant influx of new stimulus and our mind may gravitate intuitively toward whatever is new and shiny.

I call this state of mind the "curse of familiarity." Because of my awareness of something, I am often falsely under the impression that I understand it. However, I've often not done the heavy lifting necessary to examine the merits of the idea or to consider how it actually fits within my existing perception of the world. Intellectual growth results not from the accumulation of tidbits of information, but from considering and integrating it. Applied curiosity is the engine that drives this process. As Alexander Pope remarked, "Some people will never learn anything, for this reason, because they understand everything too soon."

As odd as it sounds, it can be beneficial to disconnect from certain sources of information and streams of content so that you can cultivate a more curated flow of inspiration. You get to play the role of curator of your own life and creative process. When you become more selective about where you spend your valuable attention, you cultivate the capacity to notice the subtleties of life and apply new observations to your work. This requires a commitment to the discovery process, and active pursuit of possibility. You can't just wait around for inspiration to strike—you have to aggressively pursue it by asking probing questions and mining your environment for the raw materials of brilliance.

Living Inverted

Do you ever feel like there's more work coming out of you than there is inspiration going in? I call this "creative inversion" because it feels like you're working upside down, in a world where demand drives ideas rather than supply. For example, you know that you need an idea for the 4:00 p.m. strategy meeting, but you have absolutely nothing to offer. Everything you come up with feels like a bad rehash of a previous idea, and no matter what you try, you can't seem to come up with something that feels fresh and profound. This struggle plays out daily for designers, writers, and others who have to continuously turn their thoughts into tangible value. Because of the never-ending outflow of new work, it's a struggle to stay ahead of the insatiable need for ideas, and in truth many succumb to cranking out work that fits the bill but is nothing to write home about.

The state of creative inversion is sometimes referred to as a "creative block." When we are creatively inverted, it means that our well of stimuli is dry. The creative process involves combining multiple bits of stimuli in our environment into something new. When we are inverted, we have fewer options to smash together because we've either (a) not been spending enough time seeking inspiration or (b) we need to spend more time processing our experiences to mine them for potentially useful insights.

I once asked Chris Brogan, CEO and president of Human Business Works, and co-author of *The Impact Equation*, how he's able to produce such a high volume of diverse work—writing, product creation, consulting—so consistently. He replied, "I'm always asking questions. I'm intensely curious about everything. If I see something that catches my attention, I think about how it applies to a business problem I'm trying to solve, or to an article I'm trying to write. Sometimes I get distracted while following my thoughts, but this process of continually asking 'why' is how I continue to come up with new and fresh ideas."

To avoid becoming one of the busily bored, you need to stoke the fires of your curiosity by addressing its two forms: specific (diving deep into topics of interest) and diversive (exploring possibilities through purposeful questioning). There are two strategies for doing so: establish hunting trails and develop possibility thinking.

Establish Hunting Trails

If you want something to happen predictably, you systematize it. If you want to keep your team on the same page about a project, you'd probably set up a meeting or phone call to discuss its progress and next steps. You create a system that will accomplish your goal so that you don't have to rely solely on your memory to prompt you to get things done.

Similarly, if you want to integrate applied curiosity into your work and life, you need to have a system to support that aim. You must establish parcels of structured curiosity in your life, which means setting aside time and giving yourself permission to stoke the fire of your curiosity in a way that doesn't interfere with your more urgent work. Here are a few strategies for doing this.

Keep a list of questions

When was the last time you pondered a question that wasn't directly related to driving immediate results? Are you paying attention to those little moments of "huh?" and "why?" that crop up throughout your day? These points of curiosity—the subjects your mind naturally gravitates toward—often comprise the fertile soil in which your best ideas, and ultimately your best work, will grow. Give yourself permission to *not* know things. Some people see ignorance as a point of failure, but successful people see it as acknowledgment of reality and an opportunity for growth. Posturing and pretending to have all the answers may make you appear more accomplished to others, but it's asking questions—even silly-seeming ones—that eventually leads to "aha!" moments. The appearance of wisdom is not the same thing as possessing it, and people who seek wisdom are not threatened by new or disconfirming information.

Before going into a meeting, reading a book or article, or experiencing something new, take a few minutes to consider the questions you're hoping to address through the experience. Write down a few of those questions, and use them as the filter for what you see and hear. By doing so, you'll prompt your mind to look for answers to those questions and you'll give yourself a head start on your objectives.

As you go through your day, pay attention to that little voice inside your head that sends you prompts, insights, and hunches. Note things that you don't understand, and rather than shying away from them, turn them into questions to pursue. Keep a list of questions in a place where you'll see them often. These can be questions relevant to your job, or anything else that sparks your curiosity. I keep a list of topics that I want to learn more about, and it helps me stay alert for when I stumble upon a resource that seems valuable in that pursuit.

Additionally, you may want to keep a "commonplace book," a term I first heard from Austin Kleon, author of *Steal Like an Artist*. With origins in early modern Europe, a commonplace book was a collection of quotes, recipes, or other items centered around a theme, and designed to help its creator recall important information. You may want to collect inspiring quotes you come across, articles that pique your curiosity and that you'd like to explore further, or snippets of conversation that fuel your passion or sense of wonder. Then make it a practice to frequently thumb through your commonplace book in search of new avenues of thought or ideas for your work.

Finally, consider compiling "the list." Roseanne Cash, daughter of the legendary country music singer Johnny Cash, once shared an encounter she had with her father in which he expressed concern for her lack of awareness of the roots of country music. The elder Cash promptly compiled a broad-ranging list of one hundred classic songs and handed it to her, informing her that it was her "education." Roseanne took the advice to heart, learning the songs and even releasing an album entitled *The List*, consisting of covers of many of the original songs.

Is there anyone in your life (or industry) that you respect enough to ask for a list of must-read books or articles, must-have experiences, or must-learn concepts? Compile a list, and then work your way through it, noting your questions along the way. When you complete it, move on to another topic and do the same.

Dedicate time to pursue your questions

Set aside time on a regular basis to immerse yourself in books, films, magazines, and other resources that stoke the fire of your curiosity. Keep a list of resources that strike you as interesting, and set aside time to experience them each day. I keep a "Stimulus Queue," which is a list of all of the interesting books, films, or articles that I come across throughout my day and I want to revisit later, during my study time. I also use a variety of Web-based tools to stockpile articles I come across for later viewing. I then work through them systemically, take notes, and consider how they may apply to my work. Always leave time at the end of any reading/study session to reflect on what you've read and to consider how it is relevant to your work. The next great idea for your work will probably not come from watching your competitors, but from taking an insight from an unrelated industry and applying it to your own. Read and experience broadly, and with focus on your deeper questions.

Prototype relentlessly

To prototype means to build a model, sketch an idea, or otherwise play with concepts in a way that allows for rapid iteration. You transform something that is just an idea into something that can be toyed with, tweaked, and improved. This is essentially what children do when they build worlds out of Lego or assemble machines with Tinkertoy sets. They leverage their imagination to turn ideas into rapid prototypes of whatever object they want to play with.

The industrial design and creative firm IDEO has been helping clients develop innovative products for years. One of their core principles is early prototyping, which means getting clients to play with miscellaneous objects and try to transform them into solutions to their problem, or think about it in a new way.

Tom Kelley, general manager of IDEO, described the benefits of the prototyping process in his book *The Art of Innovation*. He writes, "Prototyping is problem solving. It's a culture and a language. You can prototype just about anything—a new product or service, or a special promotion. What counts is moving the ball forward, achieving some part of your goal. Not wasting time." In other words, prototyping allows you to make progress before you even know what progress should look like. He continues, "Prototyping doesn't just solve straightforward problems. Call it serendipity or even luck, but once you start drawing or making things, you open up new possibilities of discovery. It's the same method that's helped scientists unlock some of the greatest secrets of nature."

As you consider a problem you're trying to solve in your work, how could you develop a prototype that will help you begin to explore it in new ways? Is there something you could build or sketch that would give you a fresh perspective? Are there ways you could play around with the problem, break it apart, and re-combine the pieces into something new? While it may seem immediately inefficient to take this much time "playing," you may find that the shift in perspective radically alters your insight into the core issues you're trying to solve.

Find your "bliss station"

Several years ago we were planning an addition to our home, and there was a perfect little corner spot behind the new garage for a home office. I remember making the case for it by stating, "I need a place in which to do my life's work."

My life's work. My sacred space. *Mine.*

We built the space, and I've since used it as a private sanctuary. I equipped it with a desk, a small and comfortable sofa, shelves of books, and a lot of whiteboard space. I do the majority of my writing there, and it's where I go to escape, think, and create. I thought about my home office when I recently reread the powerful collection of interviews with Joseph Campbell called *The Power of Myth.* In one section, Campbell makes the case for having such a sacred space in your life:

> [A sacred place] is an absolute necessity for anybody today. You must have a room, or a certain hour or so a day, where you don't know what was in the newspapers that morning, you don't know who your friends are, you don't know what you owe anybody, you don't know what anybody owes to you. This is a place where you can simply experience and bring forth what you are and what you might be. This is the place of creative incubation. At first you may find that nothing happens there. But if you have a sacred place and use it, something eventually will happen. . . . Our life has become so economic and practical in its orientation that, as you get older, the claims of the moment upon you are so great, you hardly know where the hell you are, or what it is you intended. You are always doing something that is required of you. Where is your bliss station? You have to try to find it.

I love Campbell's suggestion of finding a physical place where your only job is to pursue the things that evoke your sense of wonder. I think this is what I was getting at when I said "to do my life's work." My life's work certainly is not encapsulated by the work I do building a business. It's much more than that. It's more permanent. It's the space I occupy in the lives of others I live to serve, including family and friends. It's my discovery of my own self. All of this work in private then feeds the work I do in every corner of my life, like a tributary flowing into a raging river.

Where is your sacred space? Where is your "bliss station"? Do you have one? It doesn't have to be a dedicated, specially equipped room in your home. It can be a certain chair in a neighborhood coffee shop, or a bench in an untrafficked corner of a park. Wherever (and whenever) it is, make it your place to escape, think, pursue your deeper questions, and stoke the fire of your curiosity.

Develop Possibility Thinking

A second strategy for developing your curiosity is to leverage possibility thinking, especially in how you engage with your projects. This means refusing to settle for status quo ideas and instead relentlessly embracing the pursuit of great ones.

Our family loves to assemble jigsaw puzzles. (Well, to be more precise, the children and I love to start puzzles, and my wife then spends hours on her own finishing them.) There are a few strategies that can be employed to solve a jigsaw puzzle. The first method, which our middle child prefers, is to choose one object in the puzzle and work on assembling it by mining through the puzzle pieces to find only the ones that comprise that object. The second method, which my wife and I prefer, is to go through all of the puzzle pieces and identify the "edge" pieces. These are the pieces with at least one straight side, which means they form the border of the puzzle. While identifying the edges and corners takes a good amount of time at the beginning of the process, in doing so we lessen the number of potential combinations of pieces and give ourselves a reasonable starting point. Once we've established the edges of the puzzle, we can work our way to the middle.

Doing conceptual work is a lot like solving a jigsaw puzzle. One of the reasons that I believe many people get bored in their work, and fail to engage with their full curiosity, is that they are overwhelmed by the uncertainty and options. They haven't truly defined the parameters of the problem. Consequently, their approach to their work is a little like dumping an entire jigsaw puzzle on the table and setting to work with little or no understanding of what they're trying to assemble. Overwhelmed, they may give up and settle in, happy to find that a piece or two serendipitously fall together. However, with a little intentional effort at the beginning of the process to define the "edges" of the problem you're solving, it's possible to get up to speed more quickly, explore more potentially relevant solutions, and leverage your full creative problem-solving skill. When you have clear boundaries to work within, you can feel more comfortable asking extremely divergent questions and exploring initially irrelevant-seeming possibilities. Structure and freedom are two sides of the same coin. Structure yields freedom to creatively roam.

Redefining the Problem

There are four elements that can help you explore the edges of your problem: Aspirations, Affinities, Assumptions, and Attributes. Delving into these four areas can provide you with ample material to mentally "play" with your work. It may at times feel inefficient to spend valuable time asking probing questions without a certain, immediate payoff, but doing so will often help you explore previously unmined areas of thought. The best ideas often come from overlooked or abandoned corners of your experience.

Aspirations

As odd as it may seem, it's possible to spend a lot of time working on a project without having defined the true objective. Maybe an objective was handed down to you by a manager or client at the beginning of the project, or maybe you're operating with an old objective that needs to be revisited, but you've not really defined the core problem you're presently trying to solve. When this is the case, you can spend a lot of time spinning your wheels, trying to gain traction, but going nowhere. When stuck on a problem, ask yourself, "What does this want to become?" or "What would be the ultimate end, if we were to perfectly solve this problem?"

I was once leading an idea session, generating new product ideas with a client, and momentum was beginning to stall. I asked those present to think about the aspirations of their customers, and suddenly we were flush with words such as "community," "status," and "belonging." We reframed the problem to see how we could use a product to help fulfill these aspirations, a we were quickly back on track to a productive session, generating dozens of ideas. Had we not paused to reframe the conversation around these aspirations, we would have continued to crank out halfhearted ideas that didn't really move us in the right direction. Taking just a few minutes to define our aspirations immediately sparked new and valuable insights. Bringing a measure of structure to the conversation gave us a starting point from which to generate ideas.

Consider a current project you're working on, and ask yourself what the project is aspiring to become. List three to five words that describe your aspirations, then use those as a jumping-off point for ideas or new questions to pursue.

Affinities

These are similarities you notice between the project you're working on and other experiences you've had. Connecting these dots can be a helpful way to spark new creative insights or possible paths to pursue in your work.

Ask yourself, "What is this problem or project like?" or "Where have I seen something similar before?" or "Can I see any patterns here?" See if you can identify any similarities that can provide you with traction. Toy around with patterns you observe between your current problem and previous difficulties you've had.

We learn best within the context of what we already know. If we have mental "hooks" on which to hang new experiences, then we are more likely to retain that new knowledge and leverage it in future problem solving. Compare your current difficulty with products on the market, people, circumstances, ideas, or anything at all that you can use to glean patterns of similarity.

Ask "How is this like . . ." and write down all the similarities you note. Then see if those areas of similarity spark new ideas or possible new questions you can ask. Again, you are primarily looking to jolt your creative brain into action rather than allowing it to retreat into comfortable habits. Anything you can do to nudge it in a novel direction is a step toward helping you engage your problem from a fresh perspective.

Assumptions

These are the perceived limits you place on yourself and the problem you're solving. Whether through the advice of others, or by personal experience, it's easy to develop a sense of what you believe to be possible and what you believe to be off-limits. However, sometimes you can develop false assumptions that prevent you from looking in potentially useful places for ideas and inspiration. When this happens, you may artificially limit your creativity and close yourself off to valuable solutions.

If assumptions weren't challenged, innovation would cease. We wouldn't have jazz, the personal computer, or the entire field of quantum mechanics. It's the continual willingness to press against assumptions that eventually opens a crack, and then a steady flow of progress.

As you consider your project, ask yourself, "What assumptions might I be making about this?" You may uncover that you've unknowingly fallen into this rut. Spend some time intentionally challenging any assumptions you uncover, and use them as a basis for generating new thoughts and ideas.

Attributes

These are the characteristics of the problem you're trying to solve. What does it look, feel, and sound like? What are the specific, concrete words you would use to describe the problem? Once you've listed several attributes of the problem, then use those attributes as a jumping-off point to generate ideas.

Let's assume that you're developing a new strategy for your sales team. What are some words that describe the problem you're trying to remedy with the new strategy? Are the sales people unclear, ill-equipped, or undertrained? List several words that describe the problem you're really trying to solve—the specific attributes of the problem—and then use each of those words as a way to develop new questions to pursue.

If one of the attributes is "undertrained," you might add the question "How do the best sales organizations train their salespeople?" or "How would well-trained salespeople function differently?" or "What value am I trying to create by better training our salespeople?" You might find that new avenues of thought open up as you generate a variety of questions rather than just approaching your problem unilaterally. Some of the questions might seem obvious and silly, but as you persist you may hit upon one that sparks a new way of thinking. You get to the gold only if you're willing to dig through the rubble to find it.

Using these four elements of possibility thinking—Aspirations, Affinities, Assumptions, Attributes—can help you find the "edges" of your problem and help you avoid barriers to progress. You can utilize them at the beginning of a project to help you generate a series of questions and you can use them frequently throughout the project to keep you from getting stuck.

When You're Blocked . . .

For many people, the solution to a block in creativity is to keep cranking away, trying desperately to conjure up some semblance of productive thought. They don't talk about their "condition" out of a fear of being perceived as unreliable, and so the pressure builds, which only exacerbates the problem. I've learned over time that there are two kinds of blocks—conceptual and executional—and each requires a unique remedy.

Conceptual blocks are when you can't seem to generate a "big idea." You don't know how to proceed because you can't gain conceptual traction.

In my experience, conceptual blocks are not solved by knuckling down and trying to crank through the work. Rather, they are solved by asking different and better questions. As discussed in the prior section, you need to surround the problem and perceive it from multiple, diverse perspectives in order to avoid the myopic viewpoint that got you stuck in the first place. While the four A's can be helpful in structuring your thinking about the work, sometimes you just need a quick jolt to get you out of a conceptual block. Here are some questions that can help:

What am I really trying to accomplish here? Make certain that you are crystal clear about your objectives and aren't making any assumptions or conceptual leaps that are inhibiting traction. It sounds almost too obvious, but I've frequently discovered that the source of block is a lack of clarity about the true objectives for the project. Leverage aspirations, affinities, assumptions, and attributes to your advantage to find the edges of the problem.

What is this problem like? Again, look for parallel problems you've solved before (affinities). Are there any examples of problems that are similar, or is there anything you've learned from other work that could be applied in this scenario? Metaphors can also be a powerful key for unlocking new paths of creative thought. Try to compare your problem with an object in your environment, and see if it provokes new insights.

What's inspiring me right now? If you're seeking the "big idea," look to the big ideas that move you emotionally or intellectually. What is it about those ideas that are profound? Why do you connect with them? How could you apply those same core elements to the project you're currently working on?

Unlike conceptual blocks, which can sometimes be circumnavigated with a subtle shift in mind-set, executional blocks are tougher because they are typically founded upon some kind of constraint. To break through, you need to ask a different set of questions:

Where do I feel the most constraint? Sometimes a bottleneck in your process (unnecessary complexity, relational tension, and so on) can cause you to feel blocked, even if you've not identified it. Are there any identifiable bottlenecks in your process preventing you from making progress? If so, what are they, and how can you open them up? Do you need more focus, assets, time, or energy devoted to the project in order to break the bottleneck?

Where do I feel out of control? When you surrender control of a project to someone else, whether it's a colleague or contractor, you surrender your ability to directly affect progress on the project. Sometimes the state of feeling stuck is the result of having given over too much control, or not feeling in check with the progress that's being made. What would it take for you to feel a greater sense of control?

What do I not understand? Sometimes an executional block is the result of a simple lack of knowledge, which leads to stasis or paralysis. Is there an area where a little bit more understanding of the project would grease the wheels of progress? Don't sit paralyzed or spin your wheels. Identify your knowledge gap and work to resolve it.

As Walt Disney once said, "We keep moving forward, opening new doors, and doing new things, because we're curious and curiosity keeps leading us down new paths." Don't settle, friends. Don't become one of the busily bored. Stay mentally active, continue to question, keep moving forward, and open new doors each day. You never know what you'll find.

CHECKPOINT

Commit to asking better questions and paying attention to where your mind naturally wants to go. It's a challenge, because from the time we're very young we're told to "stay on task" and to "stop daydreaming." However, those little mental diversions can be the source of incredible value over the long term.

Start a log of questions, and review them daily. Keep it in your notebook, on an index card, or on your phone or computer. Make sure you add to it often. Write down anything that strikes you as curious. "How do squirrels know where they've buried nuts?" or "How does a touch screen work?" are on the same footing here. If it's something you have a question about, it belongs on your list.

Set aside time to pursue your questions. Start with an hour a week, and over time you may want to increase that to as much as an hour a day. Use this time to investigate your questions, take notes, and think about how what you've learned may apply to your work. You may be surprised at how seemingly unrelated things can be strangely similar, or at how often your pursuit of a curiosity will lead to a solution to a vexing problem you've been facing.

Start and end each day with reflection on what you've learned. We'll discuss this further in a later chapter, but make sure that your learning is not lost due to a lack of reflection. Begin each day with the question "What do I want to learn today?" and end it with "What did I learn today?"

Don't just stare at your problems. Ask a lot of questions, and surround your problems in order to see them from all angles. Use the four A's to find the edges of your problem, and play with them until you break through your blocks. While luck and serendipity do occur, most brilliant breakthroughs will result from deep immersion in a problem, and from asking the right set of probing questions.

Share this principle: Connect with a colleague or friend on a regular basis to share your questions and what's inspiring you, and to challenge each other with new ideas. The best way to stay inspired and curious is to have a discipline of engaging in stimulating conversation with others about ideas that matter to you.

Additionally, if you're in a meeting, introduce the four A's, and use them to stimulate creative thought in the group. You'll be surprised how often the introduction of a new framework will send the conversation in an unanticipated and valuable direction.

6

Step Out of Your Comfort Zone

Verily the lust for comfort murders the passion of the soul,
and then walks grinning in the funeral.

—KAHLIL GIBRAN, "ON HOUSES"

Principle: To make a valuable contribution, you have to get uncomfortable and embrace lifelong growth and skill development.

Sarah Peck was on the hook. She was among a thousand or so people in attendance at the 2012 World Domination Summit, an annual conference in Portland, Oregon, designed to mobilize people who want to be bold and courageous in life and work. Sarah, along with everyone else, had just received $100 from the organizers as an "investment" in her, and was instructed to reinvest it to make a difference in some way.

One of the speakers at the conference was Scott Harrison, founder of Charity: Water. Moved by Harrison's talk, Peck decided on an audacious goal: raise $29,000 for Charity: Water by her twenty-ninth birthday, which was only a few months away. But how would she accomplish her goal in such a short amount of time, with only $100 in starting capital? She did a quick analysis, and decided that her best bet would be to leverage two assets: her social network and her love of swimming. Sarah concocted a daring plan: if she received $29,000 in pledges before her twenty-ninth birthday, she would swim from Alcatraz to San Francisco in her "birthday suit." She immediately went public with her commitment, and started soliciting the funds.

Peck not only met her goal, she exceeded it, raising $32,398 in just seventy-two days. On her birthday she fulfilled her end of the bargain, swimming San Francisco Bay naked, with a small group of friends and family cheering her on. She later wrote about her experiences and shared a few of the lessons she learned, including the importance of putting yourself on the line, being audacious, and letting your actions define you, not your words. "People will rally behind you if you're consistent. If you're reliable. Even if it's crazy. If they can trust you. Do something, and then hustle like crazy to make it happen." Peck was moved to take action, had a spark of insight about how she might accomplish her goal, and started planning before she had the chance to talk herself out of it. Though it was an uncomfortable commitment, she acted before stasis could take hold.

While you will probably never swim naked to raise money for a charity, Sarah Peck's actions illustrate an important lesson: if you want to avoid the path that leads to apathy and mediocrity, at some point you are going to have to step outside your comfort zone.

The Biology of Comfort

I've come to learn that, left unchecked, I default toward a more comfortable path. If I don't have an infrastructure that challenges me to grow, I'll end up doing whatever feels best in the moment, whether that means surfing the Web when I should be strategizing, watching TV when I should be exercising, or avoiding a difficult conversation with my colleagues rather than confronting the situation head-on. This is because I am biologically wired to stay within a certain zone of comfort and to avoid the seemingly unnecessary pain that comes from stretching beyond it. However, to continue to grow in my capacity to do great work, I know I need to regularly challenge that biological instinct by jumping over hurdles that force me to grow.

This sentiment is frequently echoed by accomplished people I encounter in the workplace, especially those who are further along in their career. Sam Solano is in his twenty-ninth year as a manager at FedEx, an astonishingly long tenure in today's marketplace. "I've learned that I have to constantly reinvent myself," he said. "As a senior manager, I try to be a sponge and learn as much as I can every day. I listen far more than I talk, and I try as hard as I can to surround myself with people much smarter than me." When asked how he avoids the inevitable lure to coast, especially given his tenure at the company and his seniority, he echoed advice that he often shares with his management trainees. "You have to do the absolute best job you can, even when nobody's watching you. That's the best way to make yourself invaluable to your team and to ensure that you continue to grow."

The "Last Day" Fallacy

At some point, you've probably been asked "What would you do if today were your last day on earth?" While a fun and well-intentioned exercise, it's not very beneficial in motivating action because it removes any sense of responsibility or commitment to others from the equation. (If it's my last day on earth, I'm going to spend/give away all of my money, jump out of an airplane, and eat the most unhealthy, but delicious food imaginable!) Instead, when I'm with clients I like to pose a slightly different variant.

Imagine for a moment that you will have a guest accompanying you throughout your day tomorrow. This person's task will be to follow you around from the moment you wake up until the moment you fall asleep. They will take copious notes about your schedule, how you interact with your family and friends, how you engage in your tasks and projects, and your mind-set through it all. Once the day is over, this person will spend the next few days processing their observations, draw conclusions about your motivations, and compile their notes into a book about you that will stand as the definitive record of your life and work.

How would you act differently tomorrow if you knew that your actions and attitude on that *one* day were going to be a permanent testament to your life? If you're like many people to whom I've posed this question, you would probably get up a little earlier, pay extra attention to your family and the barista at Starbucks, be fully vested in every meeting, be meticulous in every task, call up an old friend for lunch, reconcile with an alienated colleague, and generally wrap up your loose ends.

Next I ask, "How does your imagined behavior compare with how you are actually living your life today?" People nearly always admit that they aren't living their life to their own standard of excellence. So why would knowing that we are being observed change how we engage? Knowing our actions are being recorded causes us to go outside our comfort zone and do what we *know* to be right rather than what *feels* right in the moment. It forces us to act rather than defer action.

We live with the stubborn illusion that we will always have tomorrow to do today's work. We hold on to this belief like a pacifier to help us ignore the uncertainty and the weight of all that's left to do. When we consider what it would be like to have our work on display, we remember that it is our actions that define us, not our intentions.

Growth is about daily, measured, and disciplined action. It's about embracing purposeful skill development and pursuing new opportunities that stretch you to step beyond your comfort zone, even when it means venturing boldy into the unknown.

Walk into Dark Rooms

All wars are won a battle at a time, and all lives of contribution are built decision by decision. As you take ground, it can become tempting to preserve and protect what you've already conquered rather than continue to press on into the unknown. After all, the more you've accomplished, the more you have to lose, whether it's in assets or reputation. The very mind-set of curiosity and persistence that enabled you to succeed is now suspect, because it seems risky. To counter this dynamic, you must willfully adopt a default position of "yes."

Dr. Karl Pillemer interviewed hundreds of people (he calls them "experts" due to their extensive life experience) who were later in life, and asked them to reflect on what they were most proud of and what they most regretted about their choices. "The experts concur on this one point: *say yes.* As far as work is concerned, those experts who were happiest about their careers can point to a decision where they were tempted to say no, where staying the course was more comfortable and less risky, but they finally decided to give it a go." He continued, "My interviews make clear that the experts who took a risk at a critical juncture were those who looked back with the greatest satisfaction on their work lives. For many of the most successful elders, the 'say yes' attitude formed their core approach to work. For others, missed opportunities proved a serious source of regret near the end of their lives."

"No" can be more than just a word, it can also be a lifestyle choice. There are many reasons why a mind-set of "no" can invade our days:

Fear of harm. We make seemingly wise, but subversive pacts with ourselves to provide ourselves with what feels like safety, but in doing so we miss the whole point of life. The safety we seek is most often an illusion anyway, because true safety is rarely a viable option. Are you gravitating toward the safest option at the expense of growth?

Identity protection. Some people would rather live with the illusion of invulnerability than risk a possible failure. They don't stretch so that they never have to know their true limits. However, this comfort-driven form of self-protection causes them to miss valuable opportunities for growth.

Love of stability. The more there is to protect, the less some people are willing to try new things. Defaulting to the comfortable choice often means missing out on a greater contribution. Are you gravitating toward stability at the expense of great work?

Ego. "No" is sometimes a form of ego, or wanting to impose our will on the world, which often means a willingness to stand by a poor choice just to remain in control. When we say yes we hand over some measure of control, because we're venturing into the unknown. "Yes" is a move from control to influence. Is your ego standing in the way?

To make something valuable is to first say yes, then sort out the details on the other side. I've learned to treat the very act of saying yes as a victory; simply saying yes to the next step, the next task, the next conversation. If I do this enough times in a row, I will keep stretching myself out of my comfort zone, and I will eventually make something worthwhile.

The musician Thad Cockrell calls this "walking into dark rooms." You may be hesitant, but you have to enter and turn on the light to see what's there. Sometimes you immediately turn off the light and walk back out, but you never know if something truly valuable is waiting to be discovered if you never enter the room.

David is a fast-rising manager at the largest publicly traded company in his industry. He was initially hired by the company as a copywriter, though he had the ambitious goal of eventually reaching the level of creative director. Unfortunately, there was no prescribed career path that would lead him to his goal as quickly as he envisioned. In fact, many of his early managers told him that he should "slow down" or "just be patient and learn," but he saw an opportunity to contribute, so he set his mind to a bold plan. He would dedicate the next few years to absorbing as many experiences as he could and to connecting himself across the organization.

"I just decided that I was going to say yes to any opportunity that crossed my plate. I also started seeking out opportunities to join 'hot' projects. If it was a project that had to do with the direction of the company, or with some new and exciting product we were building, I knew I wanted my name and my efforts associated with it."

Soon David was working more hours than he'd worked in his life, but he was also deeply entrenched in work that was challenging and innovative. Because of his "yes" attitude, he became known as one of the go-to people inside the organization. Additionally, he had built relationships with other key decision makers and had developed a greater sense of context for his company's goals and struggles.

"I suddenly had a much better sense of vision for how to help us be the best company that we can be. I also seemed to be much more valued by my manager and peers, because I had unique experiences from having put my shoulder to the wheel on such a variety of company-shaping projects."

When the company decided to launch a division dedicated to developing innovative new products, who do you think they tapped to lead it? David, of course. He was one of the few people who had the context and experience to lead the team effectively, and he had proven himself time and again to the leaders of his company.

"Being in uncomfortable environments over the course of those few years taught me to rely on and trust my instincts, and to leverage aptitudes that I'd forgotten about. I had to be resourceful, which meant that I had to use every skill at my disposal to add value, and learn the ones I didn't have. I had to figure out how to sell my ideas even though I had little organizational clout. This made me a much better employee, but it also grew me in ways I couldn't have anticipated." By the way, David was recently named to the position of creative director.

We don't grow by simply doing what's expected of us. If we stay squarely in our comfort zone, where we are perfectly capable and confident, we may never discover and develop our hidden aptitudes. David's career path wouldn't show up in any advice book targeted at entry-level copywriters, yet he has grown into a role for which he is uniquely wired by courageously occupying a unique space in the organization. Growth is painful, messy, and very uncomfortable, and occurs only when we are willing to stretch ourselves in order to accept new challenges. There is always the possibility of failure, but unless we assume that risk there will also be little chance of great success.

The accusation that keeps many people from acting on uncertain, but potentially valuable opportunities sounds something like this: "Who do you think you are? After all, there are so many people more qualified to tackle this project. Better to let someone else do it, and just focus on what you know you can do well."

Yes, there are always others who are more qualified to act. Yes, you will certainly be more safe in your comfort zone—for a while. But eventually, this craving for safety will become a suffocating force. It will cause creative death. Remember, safety isn't really an option; it's only a temporary reprieve from the inevitable. If

you spend your life chasing saf
and leftovers.

Sometimes saying yes mea
when they lead you away from
cessful communications dir
lieved deeply in the mission
years he had crafted a role
bled a team that could practically m
They worked brilliantly together, but as time passe
to feel a little uneasy in his role. "I felt like I had lost the fire that
comes from figuring something out," Mike told me. "I started to
feel a little too comfortable, and part of me wanted to experience
the uncertainty of what would happen next if I made a move. I
wanted to focus more on possibility than on certainty."

Mike knew that leaving a comfortable job would take a toll
and add stress to his family, but in the end, he knew that he
would regret *not* doing it more than doing it, regardless of the
consequences. "I wasn't sure if I could do it. It was a kind of
testing of my mettle. Even though the challenges are much
steeper than I expected, I believe that if I hadn't taken the step
when I did I would still be in my old job, comfortable and wondering if I could rise to a higher challenge. Now I know I can."

Another common lie that often prevents someone from saying yes to new opportunities is that circumstances may never be
this good again. It's tempting to think that things can only go
downhill if you make a change, especially when you're in a situation that is very comfortable. But settling in just for the sake of
the perks can mean a slow decline into frustration, and being
doomed to forever wonder "what if?"

When he was considering leaving his lucrative job on Wall

company that would later make him one of
nized names in the tech industry, Jeff Bezos,
CEO of Amazon.com, developed something he
"Regret Minimization Framework." Because he was
to leave his job in the middle of the year, he was going
eit a healthy bonus, which he wasn't sure he wanted to do.
part of the exercise, he imagined himself at age eighty, looking
back on his life, and considered how he would feel about each
decision. In an interview in 2001, Bezos described his conclusions:

> I knew that when I was eighty I was not going to regret
> having tried this. I was not going to regret trying to partic-
> ipate in this thing called the Internet that I thought was
> going to be a really big deal. I knew that if I failed I
> wouldn't regret that, but I knew the one thing I might re-
> gret is not ever having tried. I knew that that would haunt
> me every day, and so, when I thought about it that way it
> was an incredibly easy decision. And, I think that's very
> good. If you can project yourself out to age eighty and sort
> of think, "What will I think at that time?" it gets you away
> from some of the daily pieces of confusion. You know, I
> left this Wall Street firm in the middle of the year. When
> you do that, you walk away from your annual bonus. That's
> the kind of thing that in the short term can confuse you,
> but if you think about the long term then you can really
> make good life decisions that you won't regret later.

Don't allow short-arc comfort to convince you to compromise your long-arc goals. Rarely are things as terrible or wonderful as they seem in the moment.

The Waiting Game

One of my first gifts to our first son was the book *Oh, the Places You Will Go* by Dr. Seuss. For those not familiar, it's a book of encouragement for those setting out on the adventure of life. It exhorts the reader that there will be many twists and turns in their journey, but that these diversions are—in the end—the point of it all. One especially poignant passage refers to a "most useless place" called "The Waiting Place," filled with those waiting for something to happen so that they can move on with their lives.

Waiting in some form is inevitable, but it can also become a habit, a form of abdication. An excuse. It's easier to blame someone else for our failure to act than to face the deeper source of our inaction. Waiting is a less risky form of "no."

Seth Godin, author of *Poke the Box*, argues that many people in today's marketplace are waiting for permission to act on their intuition. They refuse to move until the gatekeepers give them permission. "Excellence isn't about working extra hard to do what you're told. It's about taking the initiative to do work you decide is worth doing," Godin writes. "This is a revolutionary overthrow of time and motion studies, of foremen, of bureaucracies and bosses. It's not a new flavor of the old soup. It's a personal, urgent, this-is-my-call/this-is-my-calling way to do your job. Please stop waiting for a map. We reward those who draw maps, not those who follow them."

Mapmakers are those who can effectively circumnavigate constraints in order to make things happen. We all deal with constraints, especially if we are working inside an organization. There will always be organizational charts, reporting structures, budgets, and defined career paths of some sort. The question isn't whether constraints exist, but whether we persist in finding our way around and through them.

Where in your life and work are you waiting for permission? Don't anticipate that someone is going to hand you a map. You'll probably have to make your own. The good news is that once you get moving, the terrain becomes more visible and navigable. It's only when you're standing still, unaware of what's over the next hill, that the path of progress is opaque and frightening. Say yes, then figure it out along the way.

Contingency vs. Ownership

When I'm brought in to speak at a conference or company, I typically get to interact with a nice cross section of professionals from industries in which I have little to no personal work experience. When chatting one-on-one with someone, one of my favorite conversation starters is "If you could snap your fingers right now and make anything happen in your job, what would it be?" There are two distinct camps that answers tend to fall into.

The first camp is what I call the "contingency" response. These people feel that the trajectory of their future success is contingent upon relief from constraints they are currently experiencing, and the greatest wish they have is that these constraints would be eliminated so that they could truly shine in their role. Sometimes it's a manager who they believe doesn't understand their true value to the organization, systems that don't line up with their goals, or a sluggish market that has lost its spark, but the responses are typically about getting something out of their way so that they can achieve their potential. In essence, they are waiting for something to change so that they can shine.

The second kind of response is the "ownership" response. These people seem to hold a sense of personal responsibility for the future trajectory of their career. Common responses in this camp have to do with a desire for a better understanding of how the company functions, more or different responsibility, or a greater grasp of organizational priorities. While they may still feel the pinch of constraint, their language and examples tend to be much more active than the reactive language of the contingency responders. They see themselves as owners of the problem, not observers or victims.

So I put the question to you: If you could snap your fingers and change one thing right now, what would it be? I challenge you not to think about contingencies and limitations, but instead to think of growth opportunities. You must own your own growth and take responsibility for your own progress.

Step, Sprint, and Stretch

Growth doesn't happen by accident. It's the result of intentional effort and consistent progress. You must define how you want to grow, then establish a plan to help you get there. There are three kinds of goals that help you grow: Step, Sprint, and Stretch. A step goal is a very short-arc goal (often daily) that helps you maintain forward progress, even if it's small progress. A sprint goal is a medium-arc goal (a week or two weeks) that causes you to go beyond yourself for a season in order to increase your capacity, and a stretch goal is a long-arc goal that forces you to go far beyond your comfort zone.

Each of these three types of goals nest within one another. Step goals help you accomplish your sprint goals, and sprint goals help you accomplish your stretch goals. They don't always have to co-exist, but it's unwise to set the long-arc goals without having accompanying short-arc goals to help you get there. For example, running a marathon is a great example of a stretch goal, but I would be foolish not to set corresponding sprint and step goals to help me work my way up to 26.2 miles. The stretch goal is the objective, but step and sprint goals are the building blocks. We usually reach our end goal, but fail to consider the mechanics, or the day-to-day logistics, of how we will actually get to where we want to be.

Step goal: What will I do today, no matter what?

Accomplishing a stretch goal is less a linear march to the finish line than it is a series of combustive battles. If you don't define the battles, you will be defined by them. I call these daily battles "step goals" because they help you make progress on your mission. They aren't major milestones, but are small, measured steps that help you maintain forward motion. Sequence enough step goals in a row, and you will eventually make significant progress.

Jerry Seinfeld once shared the secret of his comedy success with a young, aspiring comedian named Brad Isaac. At the time, Isaac was working open-mike nights in comedy clubs and was trying to learn as much as he could about the industry. One night, he encountered Seinfeld at a comedy club, and saw his opportunity to gain advice from one of the greats. He asked Seinfeld if he had any tips for an aspiring comedian. Seinfeld replied that the key to becoming a great comedian is to create better jokes, and the key to creating better jokes is to create more of them, which meant writing every day. He said that he kept a giant wall calendar, and he would mark a big red X on the days when he wrote jokes. After a few days, he'd created a chain. The longer the chain got, the harder it was to break. His advice to Isaac? "Don't break the chain."

The same principle applies to any step goal. Sequence enough of them in a row, and you will make progress on your sprint and stretch goals. This will help you be strategic about stepping outside your comfort zone daily, and steer you away from stasis. How can you do a little more today than you did yesterday? Is there a strategic way you can step outside of your comfort zone? How will you know when it's time to put an X on the calendar?

Sprint goal: Waging a campaign

A sprint goal is a series of step goals that extend over a season. You will sprint for a week or two, then take a break, then sprint again, and so forth. A sprint goal is designed to stretch your endurance and generate significant momentum on your stretch goal. As you sit and plan your week, consider an intermediate goal that will help you make progress on your stretch goal, one that can be accomplished in two weeks or less, and determine what you will have to do each day in order to accomplish it. Then turn the daily increments into step goals.

Stretch goal: What's the change?

A stretch goal is big. It's a major feat. It's something that will challenge you to grow. The important factor when choosing a stretch goal is that it's something you can control and measure. If you can't control it, you can't plan for it. While getting a promotion and landing a major client are valuable goals, there are too many factors you can't control. However, improving your sales skills, writing a book, learning to write code, or developing aptitudes that will increase your chances of landing a promotion are things you can control and measure, and therefore make good categories for stretch goals.

You should always be working toward at least one stretch goal, and it's valuable if you have stretch goals in multiple areas of your life. There are four key areas where you want to consider implementing stretch goals: business/work (developing skills or context for your work), mental (developing your intellectual capacity and ability to process complex information), relational (cultivating and growing your relationships), and personal/spiritual (physical health, emotional growth, self-awareness, or personal skill development). For example, you might be working toward a business-related stretch goal, like developing a certain skill that will help you perform better, while you're also working toward a stretch goal related to getting in shape or strengthening a specific relationship.

These three kinds of goals—Step, Sprint, Stretch—can be utilized for anything from acquiring a new skill to growing a company. What's important is that you focus on consistent, measurable progress, and always have each kind of goal in your life at all times. You should have a set of step goals you are accomplishing today, which should be helping you accomplish a set of sprint goals over the next few weeks, which should be leading you toward a set of long-term stretch goals.

The pursuit of goals is costly, and you can't do everything at once. Therefore, it's important to be choosy about which goals you pursue and how.

Survey your life for growth opportunities. Identify a few skills that you could develop that would make you more effective in your work. (Remember, work is any place you add value, so don't just think about your job. Think about any place in your life where your actions have an impact, whether in your job, relationships, community, and so on.)

Define your objective. Set a stretch goal. It's impossible to take ground that you haven't defined. You must know, with precision, what you're trying to accomplish. This doesn't mean that you know exactly how you will do it, but you must have a clear and concrete sense of what you're trying to do. What is your objective today? How will you know that today was a success? What great battle must be fought in order for you to know that you have accomplished something that moves you toward your long-arc objective?

Define what you're willing to give up in order to accomplish it. Everything in life is a trade-off. There is no such thing as a frictionless environment. If you want to do work that causes you to spend yourself, then by definition you cannot do that without cost. However, you can determine—in advance—what you're willing to sacrifice. How much time will you devote to the task? What other activities and projects are you willing to forgo, even if it means failure? What trade-offs are you willing to make? You can't do everything; you must make choices about priorities.

Draw the battle lines. What "enemy" will you have to overcome in order to accomplish your goal, and how will you prepare for it? What will be your first course of action? Motivation researchers indicate that those who consider in advance the challenges they are likely to encounter as they pursue their goals fare far better than those who only obsess with the goal itself. In order to set yourself up for success, consider the challenges you'll confront, and the places where you are most likely to falter, then set up a plan to deal with those situations ahead of time.

Redirect and reassess. Failure doesn't always mean defeat; it only means that you fell short of accomplishing your objective. However, those who are resilient and bounce back to fight another day recognize that nonfatal failure provides an opportunity to become more self-aware, and to reassess their strategy. As suggested in the previous chapter, keep a daily record of learning and new insights that might help you tomorrow.

Benjamin Franklin, American statesman and Founding Father, understood the importance of short-arc goals to his long-arc objectives. In his autobiography, he records a practice that he used in order to help him determine which daily battles needed to be won in order to make effective progress. He asked two questions daily:

The Morning Question: What Good shall I do this day?

The Evening Question: What Good have I done today?

In the morning, he set a course of action that determined how he would engage the day and what specific, small battle he needed to win. In the evening, he examined his daily progress.

In a similar way, when you make it a practice to focus daily on the very next step on your journey, it helps you stay on course and prevents you from wasting time worrying about things you can't control. These kinds of small-arc objectives, strategically set, make your long-arc objectives much more attainable.

Be aware: the goals many people set are less practical or strategic and more like wishful thinking, which can do more damage than good. When you wish you were accomplishing something, but aren't, the corresponding breach in character creates a ripple effect throughout your life. It's not possible to show a lack of discipline in one area without that choice affecting everything that's important to you. Making small choices to engage in hard work is what gives us the courage to do it all again tomorrow and to encourage others to do the same.

Your Vector

No matter what's happened in your past, today you established a new vector. You set a course for the rest of your life. Where is that vector leading?

There's an old story about a man lamenting that he always wanted to learn to play the piano, but could never find the time because of his other responsibilities.

"Why don't you start now?" asked his friend.

"Are you kidding?" he retorted. "I'm fifty years old! It'll take me five years to learn to play well. I'd be fifty-five by the time I become even remotely proficient as a pianist."

His friend paused, then inquired "So, how old will you be in five years if you *don't* learn to play the piano?"

It's never too late. Each day is an opportunity to begin again; to move in a new direction or to reaffirm the one you're already traveling in. If you're honest with yourself, you probably already know where you are falling short or playing it safe. You cannot chase safety and count on emptying yourself of your best work. *You cannot pursue greatness and comfort at the same time.* Commit today to stepping outside your comfort zone and set some goals to help you get there. In short, grow.

CHECKPOINT

When you look back on your life, the moments you will be most proud of will likely be the ones where you stepped out of your comfort zone in the pursuit of something you believed in. Don't allow the lull of comfort to keep you trapped in a place of complacency and subpar engagement. Think about the following:

Is there a key area of your life where fear of harm, identity protection, love of stability, or ego are keeping you from saying yes to an opportunity? Take a few moments to consider the important decisions you're currently facing, and whether one (or more) of these might be playing a factor. NOTE: "No" is not always the wrong answer, if it's a strategic choice. The important principle is to not allow your default posture to be no.

Is there any area of your life where you are staying safely in your comfort zone rather than stretching yourself to grow? If so, what are you going to do about it?

Set a stretch goal in the four key areas (business/work, mental, relational, personal/spiritual), then determine the sprint and step goals that will help you accomplish your long-term plans.

Share this principle: Ask a friend or colleague to hold you accountable for achieving a stretch goal, and to check in with you routinely to see if you are hitting your step and sprint goals. Do the same for them so that you are working toward something together. Make sure to celebrate when you achieve your goals.

7

Know Yourself

The only thing we have to bring to community is ourselves, so the contemplative process of recovering our true selves in solitude is never selfish. It is ultimately the best gift we can give to others.

—PARKER PALMER, *THE ACTIVE LIFE*

Principle: Knowing yourself will help you counter self-delusion and pursue the unique contribution you alone are capable of making.

The stories we believe about how the world works often play a critical role in helping us interpret the meaning of events. They provide a framework—a *worldview*—through which we filter our experiences. As such, the stories we tell ourselves—

and tell *about* ourselves—can be either motivating, contributive forces or limiting, destructive forces as we strive to unleash our best work. It's important that we gain an understanding of not only what those deeply held beliefs are, but also how they might be affecting our daily activity. Doing so, and then mapping our activity around that self-knowledge, is one of the keys to sustained success.

To illustrate, consider how you would respond to the following scenario: Imagine that you and I are tasked with collaborating on a project that's critical to the future of our company. We're given a month to do the work, and at the outset we agree to a fair division of labor. However, over the next several weeks, you diligently do your part while I slack off, clearly not pulling my weight. I cut out of work early, come in late, and take a few days to respond to your urgent e-mails about the project. In the end, thanks to your heroic compensation for my lack of discipline, the project turns out better than the company originally hoped for. Unfortunately, it was at great personal expense to you. You're exhausted, and not a little miffed that I completely bailed on our original agreement.

The day arrives when we're scheduled to present the project to our entire division. We're introduced, and from the beginning of the presentation I leap into the spotlight. I'm answering questions, pointing out the brilliance and elegance of the solution "we" arrived at, and generally making it seem as if I was an equal driving force behind the work. We're a hit, and after the presentation we are informed by our manager that we'll be rewarded for our efforts with equal bonuses.

How would you feel? You'd probably be pretty frustrated, and rightly so! It's an example of unfairness in its highest form.

You did all the work, and I took much of the credit, and am equally rewarded. (Unfortunately, this is not an uncommon occurrence in many organizations.)

The point of interest here, though, is *why* you feel frustrated by my behavior. At the beginning of the project, we were tasked with solving a problem, which is exactly what we did. Sure, you did the great majority of the work, but in the end, didn't we reach our objective?

The reason you feel frustrated is that there is a deeper story playing out here. You sense that some great wrong has been perpetrated when I stole the credit for your work, and it conflicts with how you think the world should work. (And you're right!) The narrative that is causing your frustration goes something like this: "*Hard work is always fairly rewarded.*" When something breaks from this narrative, you feel that there's an injustice that needs to be righted. Maybe you'll go to our manager and let her know the real story, or you'll look for a way to slip anecdotes about the project into conversations to help set the record straight. (Or maybe you'll just chalk it up to a lesson learned, and move on with your life.)

This is just one example of how the deeply held beliefs that you hold about the workplace, your abilities, and the motivations of your peers can affect your behavior. In the above example, there is an obvious (and universal) narrative playing out. You should be rewarded for your work! Few people would argue that you are wrong to feel like I have stolen something from you. However, there are other, more subtle beliefs that can influence the choices you make each day, and can sometimes stand in the way of your ability to fully engage your work.

"Recognition for work is the highest form of currency." This may drive you to do anything necessary to get credit for your work, or may cause you to gravitate toward a line of work where you'll receive the largest amount of esteem. (In the above example, this may have been what caused me to so blatantly, and perhaps unwittingly, hog the credit for what was ultimately your work.) If this is a narrative you unknowingly believe, then you might focus only on activities where you get a lot of immediate feedback and subsequently fail to engage in important but largely invisible work that has a longer-term payoff. You may also be more likely to judge the results of your work based solely on the feedback of others, and subsequently lose touch with your own gauge of excellence.

"You are worth only what you create." This is a common narrative that I discover in the lives of creative professionals, especially those who specialize in the arts, such as designers, writers, musicians, and other professions where their work is on public display. Their worth is often tied up in the things they do or make, and it's hard for them to separate their personal value from the quality of their latest project. This belief can cause bouts of frustration followed by elation, followed by depression, and is dangerous because it's an endless and wasteful chase after the perfect creation. The cycle of constantly increasing expectations creates an unrealistic bar for excellence, but contrary to what one would expect, this dynamic doesn't always lead to better results. Oddly, it sometimes leads to a failure to engage fully in the work out of a fear that it will never measure up, and because self-worth is tied to results, the deeper fear is that failure in work means failure in life.

"I have to win everything." This narrative puts you on the defensive, and may cause you to fight battles that no one expects you to fight, or to refuse to learn from failure because you can't seem to reconcile with the reality that you failed. Ultimately, it may also cause you to choose only battles that you find easy to win and cause you to fall short of exercising your true capability. There is nothing wrong with being competitive—I *hate* losing in any context, from board games to boardrooms—but you must choose your battles strategically. You cannot fight every battle, and when you lose (which sometimes happens when attempting difficult things) you must assess, redirect, and reengage rather than seeing it as a ding on your personal ability.

"The person who dies with the most stuff wins." The pursuit of wealth can cause people to do things that they wouldn't have imagined themselves doing many years before. There's nothing inherently wrong with money, but when everything else takes a backseat to your net worth, you are inevitably going to compromise other, potentially more contributive efforts for the sake of your financial growth. When someone believes this narrative, or its counterbelief, *"I'm afraid that I will someday run out of money,"* it can cause them to structure their life and work in a way that squelches their contribution.

Do you recognize any of these beliefs in your own life? These are just a few examples of narratives that I've seen affect the judgment and behavior of professionals. There are countless more, and they are not limited to individuals. Destructive narratives can also infiltrate entire organizations and cause a cultural tailspin.

However, as much as damaging beliefs can derail you, helpful and strategically chosen narratives can energize you and keep you aligned with what truly matters. The inherent challenge is to vigorously pursue, integrate, and review these positive narratives regularly so that they become habitual. In other words, you must choose an ethic to guide your choices, then ensure that this ethic is carried out in your actions. You must decide how you will engage with your work in advance so that you're acting with purpose.

Emulate Your Superheroes

One of my great joys as a parent is to watch my children as they zip around the playground in full-on battle mode. Leaping off the slide, swinging across the monkey bars, my middle child yells something menacing like "You can't escape me—I'm Batman!" However, what the wannabe Caped Crusader apparently didn't foresee is that the object of his pursuit is also harnessing special powers. Apparently, he is a Pokémon character capable of deflecting any of Batman's weapons with a single effortless motion. Their individual superpowers increase to meet the destructive force of whatever weapon the other introduces. Eventually, they each realize that they are simply too powerful for anything but a peaceful solution. Looks like it's going to be peace through mutually assured destruction. Time for a snack.

Children have no problem identifying with the superpowers of their heroes. Through the power of imagination, they experiment with what it would be like to be infinitely strong, to be able to fly, to have superspeed, or to be invisible. They mix and match powers as needed and weave them together into a complex narrative that the most accomplished professor of literature would have difficulty untangling. They aspire to be just like those heroes and to reflect what they stand for. They identify deeply with them, taking on their patterns of speech and imitating their every movement.

As we grow older, it's easy to lose touch with this childhood practice. Life becomes much more complex, and narratives become less clear. There are fewer "good guys" and "bad guys"; most people are a shade of gray. The obvious takeaway is that we are each a mixed bag of strengths and flaws. I've never met a single adult who wouldn't admit to having committed numerous mistakes that have hurt others and created turmoil. However, I believe firmly that one path toward unlocking our latent abilities is returning to a simple practice that came so naturally to us as children: We need to rekindle our ability to emulate the positive attributes of those we admire in others, and apply those same attributes to our life and work. When we are conscious of the qualities we want to emulate, they become points of traction to help us coordinate our daily activities around a set of principles rather than reacting spontaneously to circumstances throughout the day. They comprise the operating system that guides how we engage our work, how we interact with others, and how we make decisions with our focus, time, and energy.

However, this is more challenging than simply plucking desirable qualities out of thin air. You want to choose attributes to emulate that will help you become more of who *you* are, not more of who *they* are. It does you no good to simply pull off the mask you're wearing and put on a slightly more desirable one. The goal is to recognize the things you admire about others so that you can tap into those qualities, and so begin to tap into your own ethic.

There are a few clues that you can pay attention to if you want to identify the confluent qualities. As you become more aware of your motivations, these little clues will pop up like a red flag each time you encounter someone who you find personally inspiring.

What intimidates you?

I recently met one of my heroes. I was a co-speaker at the same conference, and after our respective talks, we had the chance to spend about half an hour chatting about our life and work. As we were discussing some new projects, I began to sense a sharp clarity from him about the work he was launching. I simultaneously began to feel a little intimidated by his clarity. Traditional trappings of success such as money, fame, or acclaim very rarely (if ever) intimidate me. I've met many extremely successful people without a single tweak of my intimidation meter. However, when I come across someone with extreme conviction about their work, it pushes me to the edge of my comfort zone. I think it's because I crave that kind of precision in my own work, and I feel a little like the ground I stand on is being challenged. I came away from our conversation feeling inspired to refine my vision and to better clarify my objectives for some of the new projects I was launching.

As you consider the people you admire—the heroes who define how you would like to approach your work—is there anything about them that you find intimidating? Is there a specific quality or two that feels to you like a "finger in the chest" to up your own game? Pay attention to this because it might just point you in the right direction in your own work.

This "intimidation" that you and I feel can be complex, but it often stems from a dynamic that's been brilliantly dubbed "the Resistance" by Steven Pressfield in *The War of Art*. He defines it as the singular, oppressive force that stands between where you currently are and the great work that you know you should be doing. It actively works against your engagement and causes you to seek any excuse for abdicating from the work that you know you should be doing right here and now. This leads to distraction, which leads to procrastination, then eventually to self-loathing, which further feeds the cycle until you are in a downward spiral of disengagement. Pressfield argues that the areas where you feel resistance at work are often the areas where you need to march confidently into the field of battle, because you'll typically feel it operating against you when you get close to the true work you should be doing.

I've come to learn that when I feel intimidated by the attributes of someone I admire, it's often this dynamic of resistance at work. I am being reminded in that moment of my own shortcomings, and my only two possible responses are to shrink back and consider my weakness a fatal flaw, or to take note of it as an indicator of a direction in which I need to move with my work. I've learned that I need to lean into the fear of falling short, and push through the initial urge to retreat from the challenge of having to up my game. When I do this, my best work shines through.

Shortly after that discussion with my hero, noting how intimidated I was by his extreme clarity, I returned to my hotel room, took out a sheet of paper, and began sketching objectives for a project I'd been avoiding because it seemed too large and complex to tackle. The project turned into the book you're now reading.

Make a list of five people you admire. Are there any qualities they exhibit that intimidate you? Make a list of these qualities, and consider any overlap between them. Do you notice any patterns? If so, how would you begin to cultivate those qualities in your own life?

What resonates with you?

Have you ever been listening to someone speak, or experiencing a work of art they made, and you suddenly find that your pulse is quickening, your breathing is getting more intense, and you can barely control your excitement? You want to shout "Yes!" and let them know that you agree with every word coming out of their mouth. If so, you've experienced the phenomenon that I refer to as "resonance," and it can be a valuable clue on the path to performing your best, most unique work.

In physics, resonance is a term used to describe the phenomenon by which a system oscillates more at certain frequencies than at others. Each system has resonant frequencies to which it naturally responds, and when you hit upon one of those frequencies, whether accidentally or on purpose, the system will respond in kind by resonating along with the source.

In a similar way, we each have resonant frequencies that we respond to naturally, and when we encounter them in others, their words or actions are amplified in us and we begin to resonate with the other person. This can happen in the least expected places, such as when you notice a subtle theme in a work of art, you hear someone voice their opinion at a meeting, or you read their story in the newspaper.

Typically, these points of resonance are thematic, not specific in nature. It's more about the deeper theme their words or actions point to and not just what was said. Their words struck something within you that is primal to your motivation. However, this takes some time to decipher and apply.

The best method of excavating these points of resonance and unlocking the deeper pattern behind them is to make a physical note each time you experience them. Carry a notebook with you, and jot down the context, the person who was speaking or what you responded to, and any general thoughts you had at the moment. What did it inspire in you, what did it cause you to aspire to, or what did it immediately make you think about in your own work? Over time, as you pay attention to your little intuitive nudges and responses to experiences throughout your day-to-day life, you will begin to notice patterns. You will become more deeply attuned to the qualities and attributes that cause you to come alive and feel motivated to tackle your own work.

Another way to explore qualities and attributes you'd like to imitate is to read the biographies of people you admire. Get to know their lives, the decisions they made, and the obstacles they had to overcome on the road to success. You can learn many lessons from the experiences of others, and can glean principles from their lives that allow you to navigate around the same mistakes. As you read, pay close attention to the attributes they exhibit that you would like to emulate in your own life. Try to be as specific as possible and avoid vague concepts and generalities. For example, instead of "courageous," think "willing to stand against the masses." Instead of "creative," think "willing to ask counterintuitive questions." These are actionable qualities rather than vague personality traits. Make a list of people you admire, and commit to reading at least four biographies per year as a way to explore their lives and glean traits you'd like to emulate in your own life. Take note of key moments in their lives, and think about how you would have responded in a similar situation. Consider similar circumstances you've encountered in your own life, and think about how you can apply what you've learned from the lives of your heroes to your own work.

What complicates your life?

As discussed earlier, friction is not always negative. Strategic friction is what allows you to gain traction and make progress on your objectives. However, sometimes friction can be excessive and become a limiting factor in your work. This is true when an obstacle is inhibiting progress or causing a complicated redirection of efforts. These obstacles are often overlooked by the masses because they are too busy to pay attention, or they think that it's someone else's responsibility to handle them. However, the very same obstacles can also provide a deep source of motivation in your daily work. There is probably a certain set of problems that you notice in your life that others don't seem to find quite as vexing. Great people throughout the ages have also locked onto a problem (or set of them) and spent their life surrounding and attacking it.

Do you recognize others who are attacking some of the same problems that vex you? Who are they, and what are some of the qualities they exhibit that you admire? How do they attack the problem and how is it relevant to the problems that you're facing in your own work? Are there any qualities about them that you can emulate in your life? Some of the greatest sources of motivation can stem from everyday problems.

As you go about your day, or as you encounter a particularly challenging problem, ask yourself how one of your heroes might tackle it. Consider some of the problems they encountered in their own work, and how they solved them. One colleague reported that he frequently blocked off time early in the morning, when facing a difficult problem, and imagined a conversation with someone he admired. He would explain the problem to the person, and imagine what the other person might tell him under those circumstances. While hardly a scientifically airtight means of unlocking valuable ideas (you definitely want to engage in any discussions with imaginary people behind closed—and possibly locked—doors), this exercise makes it possible to explore avenues of thought that might go overlooked until we get out of our own head and into the mind of one of our heroes. By considering how your heroes might tackle the very same problems you're encountering, it helps you think about how to apply their best qualities to your work.

Excavate Your Assumptions

We can easily become coded with assumptions about how the world works, our place in it, and what we are and aren't capable of. Over time, these beliefs become solidified and we act reflexively. Unless we make an effort to break the cycle, these assumptions can rule our behavior, career choices, relationships, and capacity for effectiveness. Often these encoded beliefs are informed by our early experiences with work, by the way that we saw our parents engaging in their work, or perhaps by formative narratives that we experience through the media. If not challenged, it's possible to go through days, weeks, months, and even years of work with these beliefs acting as unseen limitations on our effectiveness and potential.

Of course, as mentioned above, the same thing happens in organizations. It's easy for groups to fall into habitual, self-reinforcing patterns over time that limit the effectiveness of the team. Mantras like "That's the way it's always been done" or "No one knows why that's the way it is" become limiting beliefs, and curtail the attempts of anyone wanting to challenge the process and bring new thinking to the organization. Over time, this causes even the brightest, most capable people to disengage out of frustration with their inability to understand why things are done the way they are. If they want to stay in their role, they also need to settle in and play according to the rules.

In order to approach your work effectively and ensure that you are bringing all of what you have to offer, you need to develop a practice of scanning your life for these potentially false assumptions and limiting beliefs. The first step toward radical self-awareness is a willingness to explore whether your beliefs about work line up with the reality of your situation.

How do you uncover the assumptions and narratives that might be forming your mind-set? It can be a true challenge, given that many of them may be baked into your very perception of the world. But try to step outside your life. Approach it like a scientist, and include others in your quest as well. Here's how to begin the process:

Set aside time at the end of each day for reflection. One of the reasons we fall into rote patterns is that we don't stop to reflect on our day and decide what went well and what didn't. Take ten to fifteen minutes to review your calendar, your interactions with others, and your schedule for the day. As you consider each event on your calendar, consider the choices you made and the conversations you engaged in, and your behavior in each. What do you notice about your behavior, and is there anything that seems to stand out? Are there any patterns in your behavior today that seem to be recurring habits or automatic responses? What would you change about how you engaged today?

Identify the patterns. If you noticed some behavior that you'd like to change, make note of the scenarios in which these seem to come up most often. Is it in your interactions with your manager? Your peers? Clients? When you're on your own, trying to engage in your work?

As you examine the patterns, can you identify a narrative that you think may be driving that undesired behavior? Think about what seems to trigger your automatic responses in those situations. Perhaps the pattern is that you feel threatened, undervalued, or in some way overlooked. Maybe it's that you feel ill-equipped to deal with a situation. Perhaps it's that you're not valuing the opinions of others. Whatever the case, make note of the triggers that seem to elicit your behavior, or at the very least make note of the situation in which the behavior seemed to make its appearance.

Create a "watch list." Make a list of a few (no more than three) undesired beliefs that you consider to be triggering your behavior. Write them on an index card or in a notebook and keep them with you for regular review. Whenever you enter into a new situation, whether it's a meeting or a block of time to engage in your work on your own, pull out the card and consider how you will behave differently if confronted with those triggers.

The way to counter limiting elements of your mind-set is to intentionally stem their effects by reshaping deeply ingrained beliefs so that they're more consistent with reality. This must be done in small steps, and you must train yourself to look for ways in which these beliefs are triggering unhealthy and unproductive responses, through consistent reflection and measured action.

I've often encouraged teams to engage in this practice by making public the list of beliefs they are trying to stamp out, then instilling some kind of ritual that automatically kicks in whenever one of those assumptions or limiting beliefs comes to light in a meeting or conversation. An infraction might mean an individual makes a charitable donation of some kind, or buys a round of drinks for the team, but having a watch list with defined consequences helps everyone stay aware of how assumptions or undesired narratives are affecting the team's effectiveness.

Seek feedback. It can be challenging to stay on track when many of the things we need to change in order to improve fly beneath our radar, or are so ingrained that we don't recognize how they impact others. It's important to engage others on the journey of growth. Ask someone you interact with regularly to offer feedback on ways you can improve. Give them full permission to tell you whatever they think will help you improve your performance, especially as it relates to the "soft skills" of communication, collaboration, and leadership. It's important when receiving feedback to be open and receptive, and not defensive. The feedback is being offered for a reason, even if that reason isn't apparent to you. Just as many companies ignore valuable market opportunities because of baked-in assumptions, your greatest opportunity for growth is often in areas you're overlooking because they seem irrelevant to your current goals. Stay open, stay flexible, and be adaptable.

In an interview with Peter Bregman, author of *18 Minutes*, he shared an additional method for ensuring that you don't slip into a rut and drift through your days. He recommends setting an alarm to ring each hour throughout the workday as a prompt for evaluating the work you're doing at the moment. When the alarm sounds, Bregman says, he asks himself whether what he is doing is truly aligned with what he thinks he should be doing, and whether he is being the kind of person he aspires to be. The simple but profound effect is to prevent you from drifting any more than an hour off course, because you will be continuously readjusted if you do.

Breaking unhealthy and assumptive patterns throughout your day by installing "speed bumps" is a fantastic way to ensure that your methods of engagement aren't growing stale and ineffective. However, as I mentioned before, change for the sake of change is often more disruptive than helpful. The key is to find a balance between introspection and flow. Choose a few key moments throughout your day when you can pause to examine your methods, then get out of your own way and dive into your work.

Now you have a framework for understanding how negative narratives may be infiltrating your work, and that even if you eliminate them they will often return unless you replace them with something more productive. To do that, you need to define the ethic by which you will engage in your work, then integrate it into your workflow.

Establish Your Code of Ethics

At some point, it's likely someone has exhorted you to define your values. This is one of the staples of motivational advice, and typically means identifying the things that you hold dear, such as family, health, and faith, and building your life around them. However, I've found that values alone, while important, are inadequate to drive daily action. They are passive, not active imperatives. Instead of falling back on a set of passive values, you must transform them into a code of ethics—a set of operating instructions for your daily activity. This "code of ethics" is a series of words that concretely defines how you will engage in your work. It defines ahead of time how you will make decisions, interact with others, and make choices when things get difficult.

Several years ago, I felt like I was becoming a bit stagnant in my work. I found that my meetings were blending into one another, and because my work was largely strategic and managerial, there was little concrete and measurable progress at the end of each day. Sure, I could identify trends and small victories along the way, but for the most part I was leading slow change.

I realized that I needed to establish a way to define what it felt like when I engaged in my work successfully. What change did I really want to see through my efforts each day? What important and active qualifiers could I build into my life? I sat down for a few hours, reflected, and established an ethic for how I would engage:

Artistic—I would approach every interaction, meeting, and task with the objective of revealing the hidden truth or making it beautiful.

Curious—I would never settle for the first answer, but would instead ask probing questions that would help me get to the deeper truth.

Healthy—I would be a champion for the health of myself and my team, and I would refuse to compromise their health in order to squeeze out a little more work.

Energizing—I would add more energy to any situation than I took away. I would refuse to be an energy drain.

Once I began approaching my days through this lens, my level of engagement changed. I found that I had a starting point and metric for the success of my daily activity, and a gauge for measuring my progress. "Did I approach that artistically? Did I ask questions? Did I leave the room energized?" I was now proactively defining how I would engage in my work rather than allowing my work to alter my mood and my energy level.

To establish your code of ethics, dedicate a few hours to reflecting on your life and work and how you might want to engage differently. Consider the conclusions you came to when examining the people you admire, and while excavating the narratives/assumptions you carry.

Were there any themes that you discovered?

What characteristics of your heroes do you wish to emulate?

What patterns/narratives/assumptions do you want to break?

How would you want others to describe you?

Begin writing words that describe how you'd like to engage in your work. Don't self-edit, and write as many as you can come up with. Once you have a good pool of candidates, narrow it down to three or four. (No more, as you can't focus on too many at once.)

Write them on an index card, or on a sticky note, and put them someplace you'll see them frequently. I would make it a habit to pull out my list just prior to any meeting or interaction so that I was grounded in how I expected myself to behave. When I was confronted with an especially tricky situation, I would filter my response through my predefined ethic.

Is this a foolproof strategy? Of course not. There were absolutely times when I failed to live up to the code of ethics I'd defined for myself. However, the trend line was toward being more engaged, more focused, and less haphazard in how I approached my interactions.

Your code of ethics will (and should) change over time as your needs evolve. My current list of words looks much different from the one described above, because I now face a different set of pressures. It's not about achieving perfection; it's about giving yourself a lens through which to view your work and a starting point for measuring your effectiveness.

The Importance of Authenticity

You can fabricate some version of "Brand You" and march headstrong into the marketplace, but eventually your efforts will fall short if they're not truly authentic. You will eventually run out of steam, because you cannot sustain yourself long term on the approval of others. There has to be something more rudimentary and foundational that forms your understanding of your place in the world.

Jerry McLaughlin is the co-founder and CEO of Branders .com, the world's largest online seller of promotional items. He said that entrepreneurship has always been somewhat instinctive to him. "I started my first business as a kid. We mowed lawns for people in the neighborhood, and I just remember how I was amazed that I was doing work on my own, and someone was giving me money for it. It was kind of like magic. I was making it up as I went along."

For many years he pursued work that was far from what he now sees as his sweet spot. He spent years in jobs that, while respectable to others, were nowhere near the kind of entrepre-neurial venture he knew he should be in. "I think one of the reasons that I chased so many things that weren't in line with how I am wired is that no one told me early on, 'Hey . . . you seem to like designing and making things. Maybe you're an architect.' I didn't have a strong voice in my life telling me what they saw in me, and as a result I spent most of my early life do-ing what seemed safe versus what I knew was right. I saw many paths in front of me, and I chose the one I knew I could do well; the one where no one would look at me funny for doing it."

Because of his success, McLaughlin is frequently sought out by younger entrepreneurs looking for advice. He advises them, "Know yourself first, then act on what you see."

"I tell them I am in some ways like Marley's ghost. I appear before them wearing the chains I forged over the past twenty years of living a life that wasn't really my own." He says that in his experience, if you act with conviction and are persistent, the world will eventually get behind your efforts, though it may take time and will most definitely require total commitment. The first steps, however, always involve a willingness to step naked into uncharted territory. He says that we are culturally trained to look for the A+ answer, but in his experience, McLaughlin says that there often aren't answers. Instead, it's more about moving forward even in the face of uncertainty.

I used to have a cat. It was a great cat. One day I thought I would take it out to the beach, just for a fun day out. We got to the beach, and I walked it out onto the sand, and the moment I put it down it absolutely freaked out. It started spinning around, and realized that there was no place to hide. Finally, it darted back over to my truck, jumped up into the wheel well, and stayed there for the rest of the day. To be honest, that's a little like what I felt like when I started acting on my instincts and doing things that were more in line with who I really am. I was standing naked in a foreign environment, and there was absolutely no place to hide, like a cat on a beach. However, I realized that in order to really sing my own song I have to be willing to get rid of the scaffolding, and all of my emotional safety measures, and just go do it.

Don't allow assumptions, destructive narratives imposed by others, or unrealistic expectations to define your engagement today. Instead, decide in advance how you will approach the task at hand. Act, observe, then redirect. Strive to know yourself, because once you do, you will be brilliantly positioned to make a valuable and unique contribution.

CHECKPOINT

Living in a state of self-delusion will ultimately lead to wasted focus, time, and energy. You can't be afraid of the truth, and you can't allow false narratives to distract you. Instead, determine how you will engage your day according to what matters most to you, then carefully integrate that code of ethics into your work.

Examine your calendar today, and consider how you will implement your code of ethics as you engage in tasks, meetings, and relationships. Will any of these be especially challenging? Why?

Consider how you will handle any potential pitfalls or challenges ahead of time so that you aren't acting reflexively in the moment.

Create (or check) your "watch list" of beliefs or narratives that affect your ability to dedicate yourself fully to your work or negatively affect your work. Keeping them in mind will help you stay alert to their appearance throughout your day.

Share this principle: Share your code of ethics with a co-worker, someone you work closely alongside, and ask them to help you stay on track throughout your day. They may want you to do the same for them.

8

Be Confidently Adaptable

*You can accomplish anything in life, provided that
you do not mind who gets the credit.*

—HARRY S. TRUMAN

**Principle: Confidence and adaptability prevent
an inflated ego from stalling progress on your
most important work.**

This chapter is for everyone but you. In this chapter, we'll be
dealing with the effects of an overinflated ego, which of
course you don't struggle with, right? Nonetheless, I'd encourage you to stay with me and not skip ahead, because the

hidden effects of ego inflation can often be destructive in ways you may not immediately recognize.

A person with an inflated ego doesn't necessarily display the stereotypical bombast, marauding through the office demanding attention like a diva. Contrary to this narcissistic stereotype, people with inflated egos are often comfortable in the shadows. For them, it's not always about stepping into the spotlight. Rather, it's about a deep conviction that they are right (regardless of what others think), and the accompanying desire to prove it by any means. They will often do this by manipulating the conversation and bending it toward them, or by strategically withholding their efforts when they don't feel like they are being appropriately recognized. While a deep confidence is typically necessary for success, an overinflated ego can cause you to forfeit your best work if you do not feel that you are being appropriately recognized for your efforts.

In the end, your ego becomes a problem when it gets in the way of your ability to set aside your personal need for recognition in the face of work. This can play out in any number of ways, but it nearly always leads to funneling too much of your focus, energy, and time into more selfish efforts rather than into adding value.

The key counterpoint to ego is adaptability. This means cultivating the willingness to confidently bend to your environment while still maintaining a strong sense of self and purpose. To maintain traction and prevent ego from stalling your progress, you must develop the ability to subvert your egocentric needs for the sake of the work, which in the end—as you will see—is often the best thing for you as well.

Feeding Ego with Control

This morning I was upstairs packing for a trip when I suddenly heard a series of thumps from below. It sounded like someone had tossed a suitcase down our basement stairs, until, after a moment of silence, I heard an unmistakable wail of pain from our eight-year-old. I leaped down two flights of stairs, taking them multiples at a time, and was soon standing over the scene of my wife trying to console our son, who was sitting at the base of the twelve-step staircase.

After some interrogation, and realizing our son was fine save for a few bumps and bruises, we asked him what had happened. "I was trying to jump up the stairs two at a time, and I slipped and fell."

What was my first instinct? In that moment, I was tempted to blurt out a new edict for stairway behavior in our home: Thou shalt not climb stairs in multiples, nor shall thy eyes stray from the step immediately next in thy sequence of climbing.

It doesn't matter that this was a onetime event, and that our children have had no other stairway injuries despite multiple opportunities. This one incident inspired an instinct to create a rule where none had previously been required.

Why?

Our first instinct, when facing a near disaster, is to attempt to create rules of behavior that will regulate the uncertainty. It's much easier to make a rule than to attempt to cultivate wisdom. Naturally, some rules are necessary, but in this case the rule wasn't really for the benefit of my children; it was for me. I was attempting to mitigate my discomfort by ensuring that dangerous stair jumping would never happen again, despite the fact that my son had clearly learned his lesson the hard way and was unlikely to repeat his behavior.

I've experienced this same dynamic in organizational life. Something goes wrong, and the first instinct is to establish a regulation or policy to ensure that it never happens again. Never mind that it was a onetime occurrence, or that the parties involved were appropriately dealt with; a new rule regarding behavior will make everyone feel more safe. Except it doesn't. It's actually quite the opposite, because in making rules to govern group behavior we often unwittingly remove the need for personal accountability.

The problem with this approach is that soon the rules become so pervasive that they're meaningless. Rather than trusting that my son had gained a bit of wisdom from his mishap that would thereby change his future behavior, I imposed a rule that removes a need for personal responsibility and individual learning. Over time, these rules can begin to function like residue, especially in organizations. We have to surmount hurdles every time we want to accomplish something, and it all adds up to a mess of unnecessary complexity that inhibits our creative process and makes the idea of tackling a new idea or project mind-numbing.

At the heart of this desire to establish firm rules is a need for a greater sense of control. I want to feel like I can control what will happen by designing a set of rules and regulations, but these rules layer upon one another and eventually become constrictive or, worse, contradictory.

Rather than striving for control, we should instead be striving for influence. For example, I can attempt to corral my organization by instilling stringent rules or by requiring that I be a part of every decision, but it is far more beneficial for me to influence the organization to think and act effectively.

Control is all about my needs, my ego, and my desire to feel like the center of my environment. I wish to impose my will on everyone around me, and expect them to fall in line with how I believe things should be. It's not just a dynamic applicable to those in managerial positions, however. The attempt to control can happen anytime there is an exchange of value. If I want to feel like I have ownership of a situation, I can do so by choosing how I will or will not engage.

There are any number of ways that this subtle desire to feed my ego through control plays out in a workplace environment. Here are a few that I frequently see.

Playing the victim

One of the more common ways is assuming a "victim mind-set." This is when someone blames others for their inability to perform or for their relative lack of progress on their objectives. Rather than taking responsibility for their performance, they instead come up with a list of reasons why even their most heroic efforts will likely be set up to fail, and they knowingly withhold value from the organization as a form of passive-aggressive retribution. While the person playing the victim often makes it seem as if they are merely a pawn in a larger game, they are actively giving away control by refusing to take accountability for their actions.

I was once a part of a roundtable at a large creative agency, and one of the participants suggested that the reason he was unable to achieve the kind of success he wanted was that the leadership didn't allow those in the lower rungs to speak their mind on important matters. This meant that he was unable to effect change in the way he wanted, or to guide work that he was most proud of through the gatekeepers. As a result, he admitted that for many months he had been withholding ideas that he knew would be effective and hadn't really been giving his best effort to the team. Rather than having a frank conversation with those responsible, he had instead chosen to attempt to establish a sense of control of the situation by subtly holding back. His work was still good enough to be passable, but he knew he wasn't doing his best.

I challenged him that in this subtle (and largely subconscious) ploy to assume control, he was actually giving up control. He was allowing a situation, which in truth may have been unfair, to stand in the way of his best work, which meant that he was surrendering his career to someone else.

Unfairness is an unfortunate aspect of organizational work. It's typical that the best idea doesn't win and that those who contribute the most value are underrecognized while those who coast on the efforts of others are overvalued. However, when you allow the behavior of others to control your sense of engagement, you are abdicating control of your own work. There's a high cost to protecting your ego in this way.

Are there areas in your life where you are intentionally withholding in order to gain a sense of control of the situation? Instead, aggressively pursue resolution with the offending party. If you cannot achieve a satisfactory understanding, then at least you have the information you need to decide your next move. Otherwise, you're in danger of allowing others to cause you to waste years of your life fighting unwinnable battles.

Snark, cynicism, and overcomplexity

I'm concerned about the rising levels of cynicism in the workplace. On one hand, a healthy critical mind-set can help us improve our work and learn from the mistakes of others. But on the other, at the extreme end of the critical spectrum, cynicism causes us to forfeit our sense of wonder and, perhaps worse, to worry that our work will become the target of someone else's ire.

Because of this, I see many people struggling to avoid making anything that seems on the surface to be too simple or obvious. In the effort to prove how accomplished they are, they overcomplicate their work. The assumption is that complexity proves value and removes the opportunity of being criticized for being too "simplistic."

However, in these situations we too easily confuse value with complexity. These are two exclusive concepts that are not necessarily related. Unnecessary complexity can severely reduce the value of a solution by solving problems that don't need solving. The result is that we waste our focus, time, and valuable creative energy.

Why do we do this? Why do we overcomplicate our work?

One reason is that we believe that what is obvious inherently lacks value. We dismiss quick insights and familiar-seeming ideas because we assume that they can't possibly be useful. Our paranoid self worries about what others will think of us if we execute such an obvious idea. Our cynical side knows exactly what we would say about someone else if they executed the same idea. We worry about everything except the value we're creating for our clients or audience, which is the very thing that we *should* be focusing on. We can't afford to dismiss our immediate insights and first hunches.

Is there a place in your life where you are overcomplicating your work out of a desire to make what you produce appear more valuable? Is this subtle form of ego protection causing you to forfeit more valuable solutions?

Judging your work relative to others' rather than on its own merits

Another sign of ego inflation is when you judge your work based on its relative perception rather than on its own merits. You're mostly concerned about what the work says about you. When perception by others becomes your primary consideration, you are less likely to do the small things that nobody sees but that ultimately determine the level of craftsmanship in your work. Your standard wavers, because it's based on the relative standards of those who surround you. When esteem becomes your primary objective, your work will eventually suffer.

Expecting to be accommodated

Someone with an inflated ego expects that the world will bend around them rather than seeking ways to contribute whatever value serves the work. They become more focused on preserving and protecting their role within the organization than they are about engaging in work they can be proud of. Again, this doesn't always mean that they stand square in the middle of a spotlight, expecting others to bow in their presence. Instead, it might mean a quiet, passive-aggressive withholding of effort or strategic massaging of communication in order to build a bulwark around their organizational standing.

Confidence vs. Overinflated Ego

I want to make sure you understand my intention in discussing confidence versus ego. You should be certifiably and aggressively confident in your abilities and opinions. You should fight to have your work seen and utilized, and should never bow in the face of pressure to compromise. You must never allow your fear of developing an inflated ego to cause you to shrink back from the important work that's before you. The problems our world faces demand confident and competent people pouring themselves fully into their work and standing in the gap for what they believe. Do not confuse this issue. You can't be afraid to confidently draw lines in the sand.

However, you must also ensure that your need to be recognized for your work doesn't replace the *doing* of the work. Yes, you may still find success that way, at least in the eyes of others, but you may also experience regret over wasting years of opportunity nursing a bruised ego.

When I discuss these ego-related concerns with teams, they sometimes ask whether I mean they should be passive and deferential. They imagine that I mean they should go meekly through their day, never making waves or standing their ground. This couldn't be further from the truth! You must aggressively speak your mind and confidently contribute value if you want to make progress on your important work. You must develop a deep confidence in your abilities and believe deeply in what you do. The difference between someone with confidence and a person with an overinflated ego is that the confident person is willing to take a stand on behalf of the work and what they believe is right, whereas the person with the overinflated ego is more concerned with how they will be perceived and how much credit they will receive.

Here are a few subtle (or not-so-subtle) mind-set differences between a person acting from a position of confidence and a person acting out of an inflated ego:

"I can get this right" vs. "I can do no wrong"

A confident person acts, observes, and redirects. A temporary failure is not seen as a sign of permanent trouble, but merely as a sidestep on the path to success. However, an overinflated ego can create blind spots that prevent us from seeing obvious areas of vulnerability. When we start to believe that we can do no wrong, we lose the edge that keeps us alert and open to new opportunities for growth. This is when we make stupid mistakes, or we stop asking how we can take new ground and continue to develop our expertise. An overinflated ego can at times cause someone to take unwise risks out of an inflated sense of invulnerability. They don't calculate the risk because they don't really want to know the answer.

"I'm valuable" vs. "I'm invaluable"

Confidence is knowing what you're worth, and being unafraid to assert yourself in order to aggressively contribute value. Confident people refuse to be cut out of a conversation because they know they have something to offer, not because they feel the need to be involved in everything. Someone with an inflated ego, on the other hand, often believes they can't be replaced or that their damaging flaws will be overlooked because there are no other options. They believe they add value via their presence.

"Strategic compromise is essential" vs. "Bend to me, always"

A confident person isn't intimidated by contrary points of view, and is always willing to entertain them and to potentially compromise when there is a strategic advantage in doing so. They are willing to subvert their own interests for the sake of the work. A person with an overinflated ego is more concerned about what the work says about them than about ensuring the success of the project. They are willing to compromise the overall effectiveness of a project for the sake of getting the credit.

"My track record demonstrates competence" vs. "My track record demonstrates invulnerability"

Confident people are well aware of their abilities, but are also alert to opportunities for growth and see past failures as fertile ground for learning. Someone with an inflated ego feels the need to rationalize past failures or rewrite history in order to protect their self-worth. They are not willing to entertain the fact that they have failed unless it feeds their inflated ego in the present. (For example, some ego-inflated people are eventually willing to admit failure as long as it can become a kind of "badge of honor" that helps them accomplish their current goals.) Generally speaking, those with inflated egos have a difficult time taking personal accountability for failure. They perceive that they've merely been let down by others.

"I'm not explaining it well" vs. "You don't get me"

A confident person is willing to work through communication issues without feeling threatened with regard to the core idea being communicated. An ego-inflated person shifts the blame for communication issues to the other party, and thus asserts that the problem is clearly that they aren't capable of understanding the issue properly.

Protection vs. Progression

In the end, an overinflated ego is about protection, whereas confidence is about progression. A person who is confident in their ability is willing to stand up for what they believe in without feeling that disagreements are an attack on their personal worth. They maintain a beginner mind-set while confidently asserting their will in the pursuit of great work. When ego begins to get in the way, the work can become more about protection than about making progress. It's more important to ensure that credit is appropriately given, or that blame is appropriately shared, than to do the small, often unseen things necessary for great work.

Risk assessment becomes complicated when ego gets involved. Failure is not an option, even if that means backward rationalization of events to make them conform to a story of success. Accountability becomes thin, and preserving one's reputation and sense of self-worth is more important than taking the strategic risks that might lead to new breakthroughs.

This isn't limited to individuals. Jim Collins called this dynamic "hubris born of success" in his excellent book *How the Mighty Fall*. He argues that past success can create a sense that "we can do anything," and that success is seen as an entitlement rather than the result of aggressive improvement and relentless measurement of results. Sometimes this results in overextension or recklessness, but it can also result in assumed success, which leads to eventual decline.

You must develop a deep confidence in your abilities while staying on guard against the signs of ego inflation.

Preventing Ego Destruction

To prevent self-protection and ego inflation from getting the best of you simply requires regular checkups to ensure that you're not falling prey to their common pitfalls. There are a few questions that you can ask to increase your awareness of the struggle between self and work.

Where am I putting myself ahead of the work? This doesn't mean refusing to fight for what you really deserve. You don't want to be a doormat and allow others to take advantage of you. But in order to fully empty yourself of your best work you must subvert to the needs of the work your own needs for approval, recognition, and being right. This means that you, at times, may not get the full credit you deserve for your efforts, but over time you will likely find more satisfaction because you will be concerned with things you can directly influence—the work—rather than striving for control of things you cannot—how others perceive it. Sometimes when work doesn't give us what we want, we aggressively attempt to take from it what it can't really give us.

Where do I feel slighted over small inconveniences? This is a good indication of feeling underrecognized for your contribution. When you feel like you are being ignored or overlooked, or you begin to feel entitled to a certain kind of treatment, then you are in danger of allowing ego to subvert you. Entitlement can become like a noose, suffocating gratitude for even the most amazing gifts.

When I travel to a city to speak, I'm frequently met by a car service at the airport that takes me to the hotel or venue. After a few bad travel experiences, and finding that I was complaining a little too much about the hassles of travel (talk about a "first world" problem), I decided that I needed to do something intentional to remind myself to be grateful even when things don't go as planned. One practice that I've built into my travel routine (and budget) is tipping the driver of my car very well in cash, even though the tip is typically already factored into the fee for the car service. This simple practice serves two purposes: first, it is a real blessing to the drivers, who, according to my conversations with them, have to deal regularly with irritable, cheap, and impatient patrons; and second, it's a firm reminder to me of what a gift it is to have someone driving me door-to-door rather than having to fight the taxi stand or navigate a train schedule. It cements for me the importance of gratitude in those times when things are convenient, and it has had the unexpected consequence of causing me to be more grateful even when my travel plans go less than smoothly.

How can you build a specific practice of generosity into your life to help you counter the effects of entitlement?

Where am I assuming success? As mentioned earlier, one of the effects of ego inflation is hubris, which means that you assume future success based on past success. You may stop working as hard to sharpen your skills or identify new marketable opportunities because you are coasting on your previous efforts. The laws of physics apply here, however, and you may soon find that without continual effort you will eventually begin to lose steam. If you wish to grow in skill, effectiveness, and marketability, you must develop a discipline of growth and intentional disruption of your own processes. Assumptions become fossilized habits, and you eventually become rigid and incapable of responding flexibly to opportunity.

Take a moment to consider how your past successes may be causing you to ease off the gas pedal or to assume that you'll easily continue on your present course.

Cultivate a Service Mind-Set

If you approach work with the mind-set of "What can I offer?" instead of "What can I get?" it can powerfully alter the very substance of your engagement. The career expert Jodi Glickman told me that she uses the acronym GIFT (Generosity, Initiative, Forward momentum, Transparency) to challenge people to seek ways of adding unexpected value in the workplace. She challenges young professionals to understand that their main job is to contribute as much as possible, and that if they want to successfully navigate the dynamics of organizational politics, their best strategy is to seek ways of making everyone else's job easier. This requires that they adopt a mind-set of service rather than one of entitlement. In her book *Great on the Job,* she writes, "It doesn't matter how much drive or motivation you've got, if you don't share information with team members openly, share credit with colleagues readily, put others' agendas and schedules ahead of your own when necessary, and help your colleagues, then you're missing a critical business skill." She argues that this "others first" mind-set is not just for the sake of others, but that it's actually in your own best interest.

When you approach your work as a way to serve others it becomes much easier to avoid the trap of ego and entitlement. I'm not encouraging you to be a martyr. Rather, it's about confidently stepping up and contributing in ways that improve the overall performance of your team or add surprising value to your clients. Amazing things happen when you release the need to boost your ego and instead focus on the needs of others.

As you survey the landscape of your work, are there a few ways you could immediately ease the load for others or add value as an act of service? What could you do in the next week?

Encourage and Recognize Others

Another way to consistently guard against ego inflation is to find ways of encouraging others and recognizing them for their good work. When you signal to someone else that you see the value of their work, it not only validates their work but also helps prevent envy and greed from eating away at you. There are a number of ways you can build a practice of encouragement into your day, but here are a few of my favorites.

Write a note

Buy personalized note cards, and make it a practice to regularly write notes to others offering encouragement for things you see them doing well. This is a practice I utilized for many years, and I've heard multiple times that others have kept the notes I wrote to them filed away as a continued source of encouragement. I also have a file full of encouraging notes others have written to me over the years. Establish a regular time each week to jot a quick note to someone as a way to build them up. It will help you stay in touch with the qualities you admire in others, and the discipline of note writing will provide a consistent and tangible reminder of your dependence on others.

Make a call

For a few years, I had a fifteen-minute commute by car from the office to home. I made it a habit to use this "found" time in my evening commute to scroll through my phone contacts and make a quick call to someone in my work group that I'd fallen out of touch with, or who I wanted to encourage in some way. This meant that every two to three months I would cycle through all the people on my immediate team, and infuse a brief bit of encouragement or motivation into them. If your commute or schedule doesn't allow for this, find ten minutes a few times each week to connect with someone and share something you appreciate about them.

Mark a moment

Unfortunately, the moments when someone goes above and beyond in their work or offers an especially valuable idea can get overlooked as we move on to other, newly urgent things. While there may not be time (or desire) for a party every time someone does something excellent, taking the time to interrupt what you're doing to mark a moment can be a great way to highlight others' contribution. Don't be shy about calling a time-out to thank someone for their effort, or to pause a meeting for a few moments to recognize an act of excellence. In doing so, you're shining the spotlight on someone else and directly combating the need for control and a boost to your own ego.

Get Real with a SWOT Analysis

Self-awareness is an important aspect of consistent performance, and it's also critical to avoiding the dangers of ego inflation. One way to root yourself in reality is to conduct a regular SWOT analysis. SWOT stands for Strengths (the activities you are naturally good at), Weaknesses (the activities you struggle with), Opportunities (areas where you are likely to perform well if given a chance), and Threats (areas where you are vulnerable). While this exercise is often performed by organizations as a means to explore strategy options, it can also be valuable on an individual basis to help you determine where to place your focus and to help you maintain a realistic sense of your performance.

To perform a personal SWOT analysis, dedicate about thirty minutes to the exercise, and ask yourself the following:

Strengths: What unique value am I able to add consistently? What have I recently discovered I'm good at?

Weaknesses: What activities am I consistently poor at, despite my best effort? Is there a way to improve my skills in the more crucial areas where I'm failing?

Opportunities: Where do I have the most potential to add value over the coming weeks or months? How can I position myself to do so?

Threats: Where am I most vulnerable, and where do I have the most likely chance of failing over the coming term? How can I mitigate the chance of failure?

Once you've taken the time to analyze each of these elements, develop a plan of action to help you act based upon what you observe. How can you structure your days so that you can better leverage your strengths and minimize your dependence on areas where you are weakest? How can you cultivate your focus, time, and energy to leverage your upcoming opportunities? How can you decrease the chances you'll fall prey to threat areas?

Regularly conducting a personal SWOT analysis can help you stay attuned to areas where you are likely to assume success (strengths) and remind you of areas where you are likely to underperform (weaknesses). This can help you stay grounded in reality, and subsequently prevent your ego from taking center stage.

While confidence is essential to performance, it's critical that you not allow your need for an ego boost to usurp your ability to pour yourself fully into your work, even absent the recognition you rightly deserve. It is a tragedy to look back on your time and realize that you failed to engage fully and freely because your ego demanded something more.

Be aggressively confident and stand your ground, and then be willing to adapt when necessary to achieve the results you want. If you do this, you will be far less likely to look back on your work with regret.

CHECKPOINT

Ego is an especially sinister foe because it often comes disguised as justice. It's easy to convince yourself that you're entitled to things you're not getting, and that your actions are warranted because you've not been appropriately recognized for past performance. However, it's also easy to allow this sense of entitlement or the need for control to become a stumbling block in your engagement.

- Is there a place in your life where ego might be getting in the way of your work? Are you playing the victim, withholding effort, or feeling entitled in an unhealthy way? What can you do to rectify it?

- In what way could you encourage someone today (writing a note, making a call, etc.)?

- Dedicate some time this evening to do a SWOT analysis. Does anything surprise you?

Share this principle: There is such a fine line between confidence and inflated ego, it can often be challenging to discern the difference without help from others. Ask someone you trust to help you see instances in your life where you seem to be aiming for control rather than influence, or where you may be allowing your ego to stand in the way of generosity.

9

Find Your Voice

I did stand-up comedy for eighteen years. Ten of those years were spent learning, four years were spent refining, and four years were spent in wild success. . . . I was seeking comic originality, and fame fell on me as a by-product. The course was more plodding than heroic.

—STEVE MARTIN, *BORN STANDING UP*

Principle: Find your voice and conquer the fear of failure by taking small, calculated risks each day.

I used to have at least a few hours in my office in the morning before I needed to get moving. Now that we have three children, my morning time has diminished significantly. Our youngest, Ava, bounds out of bed at the first sound of activity so

I try to sneak past her and usually manage to steal at least half an hour or so of quiet time before she peeks her head through my office door, looking for a morning hug.

This morning Ava snuck into my office with an announcement: "I only have a few minutes here, because I have to go to work."

"Oh, all right," I replied.

Ava's "office" is the closet in our basement. I often see her tucked away in there with her pink toy laptop typing away for several minutes at a time. Curious, I thought I'd probe a bit. "Ava, what do you do when you work?"

She thought about it for a few seconds, eyes turned upward. "Well, I . . . I do things, and . . ." She paused again. "Well . . . I don't know. They haven't told me yet."

Ava, who spends a significant amount of time each week nestled in a basement closet typing away on a nonresponsive computer, is waiting for a nonexistent manager to give her instructions about what to do in her fictional job.

This "waiting for permission to engage" mind-set begins early, friends. We all do lots of activities as a function of our job. We have roles and responsibilities, tasks to check off, and so on. But what do you do when you *work*? What are the things that you look back on after a long day and think, "*That* was great." What is so unique to you that you shouldn't have to wait for permission from anyone to knock it out of the park?

Now the real question: How much time do you spend doing those things—the true work that *really* adds value—on a daily basis? Because that work—that you alone are capable of—is your voice. It is the unique combination of passions, skills, and experiences with which you alone are capable of approaching your work. However, many people succumb to the paralyzing forces of fear and choose to stay "close to the middle" or simply do what's expected by others rather than engaging in the small risks necessary to uncover and apply their voice to their work. In doing this, they sadly leave much of their unique contribution unrealized.

Auditing vs. Accountable

At many universities, it's possible to take a course without being graded or having the course count toward the credits you need to graduate. Otherwise known as "auditing," this practice allows someone to attend lectures without being accountable for their level of success in the course work. Sure, they're paying money for the course, but there's no chance of failing or having to retake it. You can go through the motions without facing up to the fear of failure.

Similarly, I regularly meet people who appear to be "auditing" their work life. They are present, and they may even be succeeding in their career, but they are not actively seeking opportunities to do better and more unique work. They are not engaging in the difficult work necessary to find their voice.

Life in the Shadows

"Shadow pursuits" are activities that capture our attention and give us a sense of accomplishment, but serve as a substitute for the real work that we know we should be doing. Julia Cameron, author of *The Artist's Way*, says that this is a common dynamic among people who secretly long to be artists, but out of fear choose instead to pursue careers that are closely aligned with the arts but don't require the same amount of risk or self-revelation.

"For all shadow artists, life may be a discontented experience, filled with a sense of missed purpose and unfulfilled promise. They want to write. They want to paint. They want to act, make music, dance . . . but they are afraid to take themselves seriously."

Shadow pursuits are not limited to the realm of the arts. This phrase also describes those who choose to throw themselves into organizational politics, or other side pursuits that offer them short-term wins, even if at the expense of long-term effectiveness. Employees may compete for a job not because they covet the job itself, but because they see it as a means to prove their relative worth to those around them. Someone who desires to launch their own company instead takes a job at a start-up, where there is some semblance of the experience without the accompanying risk. Someone who wants to be a writer may become an editor, helping others with their vision but never acting on their own.

Sometimes these shadow pursuits become such close substitutes for the "real thing" that we can go for years before we realize that our entire life has been built upon the pursuit of something that didn't really matter to us to begin with. We've drifted for so long that we've lost all sense of what we're really trying to do with our life. What's especially sinister about shadow pursuits is that they often don't feel like a compromise, because we can be quite successful at them and even reach the top of our field without realizing that we've been afraid all along to pursue something closer to our true ambition. Deep down, we sense the gap and know that it needs to be bridged. However, no matter how far we may have drifted off course, it's always possible to set a new bearing.

Walk Toward Your Dreams

Throughout his school years, author and illustrator Loren Long recognized that he seemed to perform especially well in his art classes. "I didn't really think much of it at the time," he told me. "No one in my family was an artist in the traditional sense, so I couldn't really see how making a living as an artist would be possible." Long enrolled at the University of Kentucky, where he chose to major in communications, though he continued to take art courses on the side. However, in his junior year he made a significant left turn when he chose to switch his major to graphic design. "I was beginning to see the work of all of these great contemporary illustrators and artists, and I realized for the first time that there are people out there who actually make a living doing these things that I also loved to do. I thought, 'Hey . . . if they can do it, why can't I?'"

Upon entering the workforce, Long went to work as an illustrator for Gibson Greetings. However, he began to wonder whether he'd really taken the right course. "All of my friends were going off to business school, dental school, and law school and such. I knew that they were all going to have jobs where they would make a great living. Here I am barely making it, and really uncertain about my future, and with no guaranteed payout to be seen. I wanted the same perceived security they were getting, but I knew that I couldn't have it and follow what I wanted to do at the same time." It was at that point that Long's father provided some much-needed encouragement. "He wasn't really able to offer me practical advice about making art a career, but he also knew that I had a real aptitude for it. He told me, 'I spent my whole life doing what I had to do just to make a living and feed the family, but I never had any kind of real passion for my work. If you can find that, I say do it.'"

Long dedicated himself to his work, honing his skills and looking for any opportunity he could find to refine his artistic style. "I've always approached my work like a plumber or a factory worker. Every day, I have a job to do. I show up on time, I sit, and I do my job. As an artist, the nature of my work is different, but I've always known that I have to approach it this way in order to be effective." After a few years of persistence, his commitment to his craft paid off. He was recognized for his unique style, and was given the opportunity to create a few illustrations for a local newspaper. As often happens, one opportunity led to another, and over the next few years his reputation grew. Soon he was invited to create freelance illustrations for several national publications, including *Forbes* and *Time*. He secured a New York agent for his illustration work, and whenever he finished a project, he always seemed to have two more waiting. From the outside, he was finally living his dream. "I remember thinking, 'I'm making it! This is what it feels like!'" he recalled. But in the midst of experiencing the recognition and success he'd long desired, Long began to grow tired of the pace he had to maintain just to be able to feed his family as a freelance artist. "I kind of wore down from the rat race. I didn't know how long I would be able to sustain that pace. I began to realize that what I thought I wanted wasn't really what I wanted."

Around that time, he began receiving manuscripts from his

agent for soon-to-be-published young-adult books in need of cover art. As he read the books, Long began to feel a deep affinity for the stories. Something resonated, and he got the sense that all of his previous work experience was somehow pointing him to this opportunity. "It was like a light went off in my brain, and I suddenly thought, 'That's it! I'm a storyteller!'

"I'd always heard stories of others who knew they wanted to be an artist since they were five years old. Because of that, I spent much of my early career feeling like I was so far behind everyone else. I was thirty-nine years old before I discovered that my real gift is storytelling, but I think that all of my experiences early in life helped me uncover that." Long began doing cover illustrations for young-adult novels, which eventually led to the opportunity to illustrate a few children's picture books. He knew that after years of circling it, he had finally landed in his sweet spot.

In the decade since discovering his love for story, Long has experienced remarkable commercial success writing and illustrating picture books, and working with notables such as Madonna and President Obama. Long said that the high point of his career thus far was being chosen to illustrate a new edition of *The Little Engine That Could.*

It cost Long several years of his life and a lot of experimental energy to finally discover his voice, but in the end, he says that the methodical process he followed has been invaluable.

"I walked toward my dreams. It wasn't a run, or a skip, it was a deliberate walk. A slow walk. I wasn't expecting to get there today or tomorrow, but I knew that if I was intentional and enjoyed the scenery along the way, it would make the journey much more meaningful in the end."

Many people who discover their voice seem to do so via the slow, layered manner that Long valued so much. It's rarely a linear path, but instead is the culmination of a lifelong process of observation, course correction, and risk-taking that eventually leads to the recognition of a valuable contribution.

Follow the Arrows

One of the most celebrated shows currently on public radio is *Radiolab*, the brainchild of Jad Abumrad and Robert Krulwich. The show explores the oddities of science and psychology by weaving expert interviews into an entrancing soundscape. The popularity of *Radiolab* has grown exponentially over the past few years due to its stimulating content and signature sound, and in 2012 Abumrad was awarded a MacArthur Fellowship, given in recognition of those who "show exceptional merit and promise for continued and enhanced creative work."

When encountering a successful venture like *Radiolab*, the tendency is to think that it was launched with a crystal clear vision. What's fascinating is that, according to its founders, the show has been a multiyear process of trial, error, and intuitive leaps. Abumrad shared in detail how *Radiolab* found its voice in an article on Transom, a public radio website. Apparently, there was little clear indication from the beginning about what the show was going to be, and certainly no impending sense of greatness.

"The idea that this program could be its own thing literally did not feel like a possibility for over a year. And it happened in tiny moments that I could have never predicted," Abumrad wrote. He explained that the nonlinear process of unlocking

Radiolab's eclectic vibe was experimental, but that there were small signs along the way that indicated which direction they should take the project. One night, Abumrad was experimenting with sounds and edits and came across a combination that resonated. "I cannot tell you WHY that collection of noises was important. But it was the first thing I'd heard that I was like . . . hey, that's not bad. I think I might hear myself in there somewhere. It was like being lost in the dark and then an arrow appears. A pointing arrow; placed there by your future self, that says, 'Follow me.'"

Abumrad explains that in the early days of *Radiolab* a lot of thought was given to what kind of host he should be, and how the show should be structured in order to best appeal to the typical public radio listener. Imitating shows that were already popular would have been the safer route, but instead they chose to blaze a new trail by infusing unexpected audio effects, and interviews that featured quick cuts back and forth between the interviewer and the subject. Initially, this was met with significant resistance from the audience. In fact, when the show finally got its big break, a one-week slot normally filled by *Fresh Air*, the response from the public was brutal. Listeners didn't know how to respond to *Radiolab*, because it was so different from anything else they'd heard. Despite the turmoil of all of this public experimentation, much of which Abumrad now calls "embarrassing," it was a necessary step that eventually enabled its founders to stumble down the path that has since put *Radiolab* in its own elite class.

It was the willingness to face the possibility of rejection that eventually led to a discovery of something unexpected and incredibly valuable. There was no guarantee of success. Certainly many others who have tried something new on the radio have failed magnificently. However, few succeed in being remarkable without the willingness to embrace the potential of failure.

Just like in the examples above, you will discover your voice through tiny clues that become apparent over time, and as you follow them and apply what you learn to your work. Here are a few ways to begin that process.

Plan for experimentation

When you're under pressure to produce quick results, it's unlikely that you feel the freedom to experiment. It's also unlikely that your manager will be willing to put up with last-minute divergences. However, if you are intentional about adding time to experiment into your workflow, you can take advantage of the loose, unexpected connections that often lead to better ideas.

Set aside some time every week to play with ideas and toy with possibilities. It's important not to set expectations for this block of time. Instead, see it as an opportunity to develop your understanding of a problem or a project that you care about. Prototype, play, and explore its boundaries. Ask "What am I *really* trying to do?" or "Can I make this less complex?" Creating a predictable structure for experimentation will alleviate the sense that you're not taking enough risks in your daily work.

Apply peripheral aptitudes to your problems

It's easy to get into a rut when you do similar work each day. Over time, you learn what's effective, and you tend to stay in that safety zone because it's the way to achieve predictable results. But over time, these methods can become stale, and you can lose your passion for your work. Your methods are too familiar and you've lost your sense of urgency.

One way to combat this mind-set is to apply peripheral aptitudes to the work. There are things that you do well that may seem irrelevant to the problems you're working on, but with a little thought they can be applied to the problem to help you explore potential new solutions. Jad Abumrad drew upon his years of experience as an audio editor and musician in creating *Radiolab*'s distinctive sound. What skills have you previously deemed irrelevant that might be helpful in your current work? How can you apply them in order to unlock a unique perspective or open new paths of exploration?

Open your eyes

There is more happening in your mind than is apparent on the surface. Something you experience may cause a flash of intuition, but this burst of insight will quickly fade if you do nothing with it. You need to pay attention to these moments of inspiration and follow—at least mentally—where they lead, even if it seems impractical in the moment. This doesn't mean being reckless with your attention and following every whim, but being willing to at least suspend your assumptions long enough to vet the merits of an intuitive ping.

What do you already suspect to be true, but are ignoring because it seems impractical on the surface? You will never do your best work until you learn to hone and trust your instincts, then develop the courage to take small steps in the right direction.

Great work results when you stop doing only what you *know* you can do and instead begin pursuing what you believe you *might* be able to do with a little focused effort.

Take a few minutes to make an inventory of your most important work, and then spend some time considering each project. Are there hunches you have about the direction of these projects that you're ignoring because you're afraid of where they might lead, or of what they might cost you? It's often easy to ignore prompts and instincts because of a fear of the effort involved to act on them. Have you been ignoring any intuitive nudges? If so, what are you going to do about it?

Do the obvious

Derek Sivers is the founder of CD Baby, an online retailer that helps independent musicians sell their music, and the author of *Anything You Want.* In an article on his website, he shared that one of the struggles he's experienced over the course of his career is that other people's work always seems to be intricate and innovative compared with his. "I never would have thought of that. How do they even come up with that? It's genius!" Sivers said that in spite of his inclinations, he continued quietly going about his work and making the things that he felt compelled to make, even though most of them seemed too obvious to him. Sivers was surprised when other people began contacting him and remarking about how inventive his work is and how they never could have come up with such ideas.

Ideas that seem obvious to you may be incredibly profound to others, but you may be inclined not to share them because of a fear that they will be perceived as too shallow.

Are you holding back insights or actions because they seem too obvious to you? Brilliant work doesn't need to be complex. Sometimes the deepest truths are hiding in plain sight.

In order to discover and act on your voice, you need to develop the capacity to pay attention to the little clues. Don't worry that society tends to celebrate stories of overnight success even when there's no foundation to sustain it. Great work, like a healthy financial portfolio, takes time to mature. Your best work will emerge with patient attention, time, and strategic action.

Notice, Then Act on What You See

I often use the phrase "cover bands don't change the world" to describe the need to pursue a unique voice rather than simply imitating others. A cover band plays other people's music, and often fills venues and makes money, and may even provide good entertainment. However, when a better cover band comes along, one that plays slightly better versions of the same music, it's out of a job because there wasn't anything unique about it. Cover bands are often quickly forgotten, but the music lives on.

This doesn't mean that imitation is always wrong. In fact, imitation is a key part of early growth and development as you are discovering your voice. You imitate others in order to build the skills and platform you need to perform at a basic level of competence. However, you cannot rely on imitation forever as a shortcut to success, or your work will be hollow, and without a foundation. In order to add lasting, meaningful value, you must begin at some point to take risks and to experiment with your own form of expression. Your understanding of how best to do that will develop slowly as you find a better context for what you're really good at. This happens when you take small, daily calculated risks in how you approach your work.

Start now, but don't rush. Walk slowly, and you'll discover your voice along the way.

CHECKPOINT

Your most brilliant, unique work will result from applying your voice. You will discover your voice as you take small, calculated risks to experiment. Try new ways of engaging your work, and learn to follow your intuition.

What small risk can you take today in your work to experiment with finding your voice?

What's something that you've been reluctant to act on because it seems too obvious to you, but will share with others today?

Is there an intuition you've had, but haven't acted on or applied to your work? What's the next step you can take to act on it?

Share this principle: Ask someone you trust what aptitudes they notice that seem to be unique to you. Ask them where you seem to add the most value. Then, if they're open, share the same with them.

10

Stay Connected

Develop an interest in life as you see it; the people, things, literature, music—the world is so rich, simply throbbing with rich treasures, beautiful souls and interesting people. Forget yourself.

—HENRY MILLER

Principle: Establishing genuine connections with others will prevent guardedness from infecting your life.

We are not wired for isolation. From the earliest moments of our lives, we grow, learn, and come to understand our place in the world through our interactions with others. We need other people to help us stay aligned and to bring out the best in us. But relationships can be uncomfortable and challenging at times. It's easy to slip into guardedness and close ourselves off from the world when dealing with the messiness involved in navigating expectations, misunderstandings, and collaborative disagreements. This is especially true when we are busy or feel like we don't have the time or emotional bandwidth to deal with the complexity of relationships.

However, closing ourselves off to others—especially in hectic times—is the worst thing we can do. When we disconnect or become guarded, we reduce the potential for serendipitous insights and connections that often come through unexpected interactions with others, and we also limit our own ability to stretch outside our relational comfort zone, which is the very thing that often leads to the discovery of new insights about our abilities and preferences.

Contrary to the fabled lore of the lone genius slaving away in their studio loft, occasionally gracing the public, then returning to their space to crank away at their masterwork, most of the great work that's accomplished is done in the context of a community. Very few people are able to stay aligned and engaged without others in their life to help fuel their passions.

Relationships—especially in the workplace—take effort, and to stay connected demands that we build practices to help us engage with purpose. I wrote about some of the more tactical practices you can implement to stoke the fires of your relationships in *The Accidental Creative*, but even if you have these practices in place, it's still possible to allow your connections with others to remain shallow and without the kind of honest urgency that forges trust, commitment, and effectiveness.

There are two common mistakes that lead to decreased effectiveness and regret: avoidance and squashing conflict.

Avoidance

Because many of our relationships are ongoing and we have regular, predictable interactions with the same people, it's easy to defer important conversations to a more convenient time. This is especially true when the topic of conversation makes us uncomfortable, such as when there is tension to be resolved or when there is no urgent reason to have the conversation, such as when you have an idea that's not tied to a current project. When you defer important conversations, you drive a wedge into your relationships and only increase the likelihood of challenges down the road.

Avoidance is a common tactic in the face of uncertainty. We may instinctively do it to defer dealing with a relationship, but that tends to create even more damage. It's easy to fill that gap with invented stories or assumed motives, so in the long run, *not* discussing an uncomfortable subject can do more harm than confronting it head-on.

You need to have a structure in your work rhythms to help you "clear the decks" and engage in these important, though not urgent, conversations frequently so that you are freed up to do your best work.

Squashing Conflict

There's a false belief in many organizations that tension and conflict are signs of an unhealthy team. In many cases, this couldn't be further from the truth! An effective team consists of people willing to fight for their ideas, challenge others when necessary, and stand their ground when confronted. In the end, however, those same people must be willing to bend to the ideas of others and submit to the decisions made by the leader, knowing that they can't win every battle. Unfortunately, managers are often uncomfortable with these fits and spurts and attempt to squash team conflicts so as to preserve the peace. There's a false belief that tranquillity equals health, but a tranquil team is often a sign of imminent death because it may mean that no one cares enough to make waves.

Sarah Young is one of the partners of National Public Relations. Over the past several years the marketing-communications company has seen remarkable growth. I conducted a workshop for the office in Halifax, Nova Scotia, and came away so impressed by its culture that I probed her about their methodology. "We really wanted to create a collective," she told me. "Hiring for diverse viewpoints is the best thing for the long term, even if it's painful in the short term." It's painful, she says, because you have to deal with strong personalities and divergent opinions, but if you're able to navigate those rough waters, you come through with a much better chance of delivering a brilliant result. "Even when it gets challenging because of a disagreement or argument on the team, there is a fierce sense of protection for the culture. There is a strong sense of 'we,' because people have learned that we can do so much more when everyone is free to speak their mind."

The same freedom comes when we are willing to directly address differences of opinion in our one-on-one relationships. There is a tendency to pursue harmony rather than create an environment where speaking your mind is the norm, and a temptation to prematurely squelch conflict before there's been a chance to work through it. Instead, we should be comfortable pursuing resolution with humility and confidence. This goes a long way toward preventing regret later on and toward helping us focus on our work instead of awkward, outstanding conflict that we know we'll have to deal with eventually.

In a mid-1990s interview, just prior to returning to Apple, Steve Jobs shared a story about an experience he had as a youth that echoed his beliefs about how healthy teams should function. One day a neighbor invited Jobs into his garage, where he revealed a rock tumbler. He asked Steve to go into the backyard and collect a few rocks, and then the neighbor took the rocks, which were normal ones with rough edges, and placed them into the tumbler along with some grit. After flipping the switch to start the machine, he told Jobs to return the next day. The following day, the neighbor stopped the tumbler and removed "amazingly beautiful polished rocks. The same common stones that had gone in, through rubbing against each other like this [smacking hands together], creating a little bit of friction, creating a little bit of noise, had come out these beautiful polished rocks." Jobs went on to explain how this metaphor informed how he believed great products were made. He said, "It's that through the team, through that group of incredibly talented people bumping up against each other, having arguments, having fights sometimes, making some noise, and working together they polish each other and they polish the ideas, and what comes out are these beautiful stones."

I always challenge leaders to encourage dissent and foster discontent on their teams. This doesn't mean provoking fights for the sake of it. Rather, it means demanding that team members speak their mind, and then highlighting points of disagreement so that everyone is clear about the argument being made by all sides. Then I encourage them to persist in prodding people to fight for their position until there is clearly a winning idea. To be effective, we must resist the urge to censor the conversations—no matter how tense—that might lead to breakthrough ideas.

Running Toward Others

To ensure that you are engaging in your life and work in such a way that you are maximizing your contribution, you must pursue relationships with the same level of diligence and urgency that we've discussed throughout the earlier chapters of this book. You cannot operate by default; you must instead have a plan for how you will regularly scan your life for open loops, and how you will intentionally pursue relationships that keep you on track with your goals. There are two strategies in the remainder of this chapter to help you do this: Find Mirrors and Use Probing Conversations.

First, let's all agree that relationships are tricky because they always involve diverse interests, objectives, and personalities, and there are no surefire ways to ensure relational success, because you are always at the mercy of these unknowns. Second, and you've probably noticed this is a theme throughout the book, you must approach your relationships with the attitude of "What can I offer?" rather than "What can I receive?" If you engage in relationships from a posture of generosity, with a genuine desire to serve the needs of others while simultaneously seeking a better understanding of yourself and your abilities, it will be a win for everyone. The more you are able to give, the more you will learn about yourself and your own limits and potential.

Find Mirrors

Just as a mirror allows you to see your true appearance, other people in your life can serve to help you see beyond your assumptions and blind spots. No matter how confident you are in your abilities, there will come a time when you are uncertain of the next step. In these situations, it's important to have someone who can help you stay aligned and remind you of what's truly important. We all need these kinds of mirrors in our life.

Are there people in your life who have full permission to speak truth to you about what they see? These kinds of relationships are not easy to cultivate, because you must find people you trust and respect, and who you know will speak out of a genuine concern for your best interests rather than as a way to influence you toward their own. However, if you can identify a few people to play this role for you, it can provide you with a tremendous amount of confidence because you know that others are also watching out for you.

Here's how to begin implementing this practice.

Identify two people to play the role of mirrors

They should be people you regularly encounter in the course of your day, and whom you both trust and respect. Ideally, they are people on your team or in your workgroup, though as long as you see them often, they can fill the role. Also, I'd encourage you to play the same role for them. By doing this, you keep one another accountable for living up to your personal standards of excellence.

Identify a few specifics you'd like them to watch for

In Chapter 7 we discussed the importance of self-awareness, and you were challenged to establish an ethic for how you will engage your work. You can ask the mirrors in your life to evaluate how well you are living out your ethic. For example, if you want to bring a lot of energy to the workplace, they can help you identify times when you are dragging things down. They can also encourage you in the areas where you are doing well at living up to your standards. Regardless of what you ask your mirrors to keep a watch over, make certain that they feel complete freedom to speak to you about anything they believe is contrary to how they think you'd want to be engaging in your work. You want them to have the ability to highlight potential issues before they become damaging, especially if they are things that you may be overlooking.

Set up regular time to connect

Establish a regular time to get together with your mirror to chat about how work is going, discuss what you're seeing, and challenge and encourage each other in your work. This will provide a necessary sense of urgency to watch for those key issues you're accountable for, and will also help you discuss ways of getting better at your work.

I'd recommend getting together with your mirror(s) once per week and having a conversation about how you're doing, what you'd like them to be watching for you, and how they can best help you stay aligned with what's critical. Make sure that you do your homework ahead of time so that you know what to ask. Don't waste the other person's time by not preparing for your meeting.

Be ruthlessly honest

This practice falls apart if courtesy supplants raw and direct communication. You must be willing to speak the truth as you see it, and to receive it from the other person even when it's uncomfortable to hear. Nobody wins when you shape the truth to make it more palatable. Direct and aggressive honesty is the salve that consistently heals avoidance and self-delusion.

Beyond having your mirrors watch how you're engaging your work, I'd also encourage you to share your goals and ambitions with them, and ask them to hold you accountable for taking meaningful action each week. When you know that someone will be probing to see if you've taken action, it tends to kindle urgency on long-arc projects that are currently collecting dust.

Adjust regularly

Again, the goal is to have someone keep you aligned with what's important to you and what you think you need to be focusing on, but this emphasis will definitely change from season to season. Make sure that you are regularly checking in with your mirrors to let them know what you'd like them to be watching for you. Your mirrors serve as "outposts" who can show you where you may be falling short of your intentions.

Remember that something that seems obvious to you might be profound to others. Having a mirror in your life can help you hone your intuition and keep your focus, time, and energy in the right place.

Use Probing Conversations

Over the past few years, I've spent quite a bit of time with teams, walking them through how to have conversations about their most critical work. One would think that a skill as basic as simply talking to one another wouldn't need special attention, but I'm often astounded at how little team members actually communicate beyond the bare essentials. Teams are often great at talking about tasks and strategy, but abysmal at discussing the intangible factors that deeply affect their workflow. It's such a common malady within organizations that I had to distill many of the more common frustration points into five areas of conversation that can bring better clarity, focus, and trust to the team.

The five conversations are designed to countermand the "assassins" of creativity. I call them this because they infiltrate any organization that depends on mental collaboration and destroy the culture and drive of the team. There are three assassins that the conversations work against.

Dissonance

This is a term I use to describe when things just don't seem to "add up" within an organization, or when there is a break between what's being said on a leadership level and what's actually being rewarded on a tactical level. When this happens, there is an obvious breakdown between what we say is important and what we actually act upon, and it can greatly affect the motivation of team members. Worse, it can erupt into a break between what we say we're trying to do organizationally and what we actually set up our systems to accomplish. When this becomes the norm, it can be challenging for team members to engage in the work because it's difficult to know where the edges are or how to discern success from failure.

This is destructive because our minds are wired to solve patterns. In fact, the creative process is simply the resolution of dissonance by the process of forging meaning out of seemingly incongruent bits of information. However, our minds don't always understand the difference between a "good" problem and a "bad" problem, so when there is unhealthy dissonance in our work environment, our minds can waste a lot of energy trying to solve ancillary problems rather than devoting that energy to solving the problems we're really being paid to solve.

Dissonance can easily creep into relationships and cause misunderstandings, hurt, and unnecessary relational tension. Simply having a discipline of intentional conversation can relieve a lot of this tension.

Fear

We tend to think of fear as terror or shock, but in this context it means that we are paralyzed with inaction because the perceived consequences of failure outweigh the perceived benefits of success. This means that we are unlikely to try new things, take a relational risk, or experiment with an idea out of a concern that we will pay a high price for failure. However, in many cases this fear is largely unwarranted and is nothing but a figment of our imagination. Fear thrives mostly in places where it's not discussed. If fear becomes a regular part of conversation, then it is less likely to gain a foothold in your life or organization, so having a structured conversation around it is an effective way to prevent it from unknowingly suffocating your engagement.

Expectation escalation

Expectations continue to rise, and most of us are being asked to do more with less. However, this can have an unfortunate and unseen effect on our engagement. When this week's performance becomes next week's baked-in expectation, it can be challenging to get excited about your work. After all, who wants to climb a mountain in record time only to find a taller one in front of them?

Expectation escalation is not just about the rising tide of organizational demands. It can also be a psychological trick that we play on ourselves when the reality is less than clear. When there is silence around expectations, we will sometimes fill the gap and artificially escalate our expectations beyond even where the organization would set them. When this happens, we are in danger of overextending ourselves or venturing off into territory no one expects us to explore. One organization I worked with mentioned that there were various "phantom rules" that existed throughout the organization that many people referenced over time, but that were in no way a part of the organization's true expectations for employees. When they began dragging these unwarranted expectations into the light through intentional conversation, they were able to dismantle them and put them in the past.

Having clarity around true expectations is essential to a healthy, functioning work life. However, assumptions will fill the void if you are not intentional about seeking (and giving) a clear understanding of your true demands.

The five conversations below will help you seek the information you need to countermand these three assassins, but they won't occur without a little effort. Healthy, well-functioning relationships don't happen by accident. They result from consistent effort, argument, celebration, and resolution. We grow together as we engage in meaningful work, and especially as we engage in purposeful conversation about what the work means to us.

There are a few ground rules to engaging in these five conversations. First, do not steamroller others. This is about building relationships, and relationships are founded upon empathy, trust, and commitment. If we're going to have these conversations, we must be committed to the results, even if they're not what we wish for. We have to be willing to hear the truth and act on it even when we dislike it.

Second, these conversations will work best if you have them both on a team level and on an individual level. Some team members might not feel comfortable expressing themselves in a larger group, but they might have insights that can help you engage in a more healthy way if you give them space to talk. You need to formalize your conversations and not just wait for the opportune time to occur.

The Clarity Conversation

This conversation is designed to bring alignment and combat dissonance. It is your responsibility to ensure that you have the information you need to do your work; you can't wait around for someone to deliver it to you. Often, people are afraid to ask questions in order to clarify objectives, because they think doing so will make them look incompetent or out of touch. This is unfortunate, because it's impossible to accomplish something that you can't define. In order to be effective in your work, you must understand what it is you're trying to do. Many people and teams waste unnecessary energy doing work that was never asked of them in the first place.

If you are a leader of an organization, these conversations are especially crucial. Much of the tension on teams, especially on collaborative creative teams, results from a lack of understanding of the work or a general unwillingness to engage with one another and seek clarity. This tension could be resolved and much time could be saved if teams were simply willing to make a discipline of asking a few key questions. Here are a few that you can ask yourself (and your manager, or your team) in order to gain better clarity.

How does what I'm doing tie in to why our company exists?

A lot of confusion and frustration stems from a lack of understanding of how the daily tasks and projects align with the overall objectives of the organization. It's maddening to me how many organizations agonize over making the right hires and spend so much time trying to get employees in the right roles, but then refuse to regularly provide context for those brilliant people about the larger objectives of the organization so that they can be fully utilized in their work. As a result of this failure, many people waste time scratching their heads trying to gain an understanding of how their work ties in to the organization's larger reason for being.

As a team leader, one way to ask this question would be: "Is there anything we're doing right now that seems out of character for us?" Step back and allow the conversation to ensue. Don't get defensive and don't feel the need to argue. This is not about being right; it's about discerning and identifying misunderstandings or areas of confusion within the team. Similarly, if you discern that there is something out of character happening on your team, don't hesitate to ask your manager about it. Don't allow a small misunderstanding or misalignment to drive a wedge between you and your effectiveness. There may be things you can't be told for any number of reasons, but make every effort to seek the information you think you need to engage in your work.

Can you clarify the objectives once more?

Are you clear about what's expected of you? Is there anything you're unclear about? Sometimes people won't speak up because they assume that they're the only person who doesn't get it. No one wants to appear like they're a step behind everyone else, but the only way to ensure that you're on the right path is to make sure that you're solving the right problems. If you are uncertain, don't hesitate to ask someone to help you clarify what you should be doing. The more you and your team validate the act of asking questions, even silly-seeming ones, the more trusting and aligned your culture will become.

Clarity is critical to creating a healthy team, and it's essential to doing your best work each day. It's almost impossible to define your battles if you can't identify the front lines. The clearer we are about the problems we're trying to solve, the more effective we will be in the long run. Be clear and ordered about your objectives so that you can reserve your creative energy for the messiness of exploring those problems.

The Expectations Conversation

Similar to how we can become less clear about our objectives over time, our understanding of the expectations of others can also devolve. When this happens, it's easy to fill the gaps with our own assumptions about what's expected of us, and end up focusing on the wrong things. When others fall short of our unspoken expectations, this can also get in the way of a healthy relationship, or we can similarly fail to meet the unspoken expectations of others. Once these expectations are out in the open, it eliminates the uncertainty and ambiguity of what's expected and creates a culture of accountability.

Here are a few questions you can ask to help clarify expectations within organizations. These can work both in a peer-to-peer collaborative relationship or in a relationship in which you are managing another person. In either case, the objective is to clarify each person's expectations so that there is no misunderstanding or room for misinterpretation.

Do you know what's expected of you?

When you're working closely with someone else, it's important that each of you regularly shares what's expected of the other. It's especially important in relationships where you are used to working together and bad habits or assumptions are likely to creep into your process. On a regular basis, simply ask the other person if they know what you expect from them and when, and if they have any questions about those expectations. Once you do this, it becomes difficult for the other person to claim they didn't know what they were supposed to do, or to say that there was a misalignment. Again, the goal is to bring expectations into alignment and ensure that everyone is focusing their energy in the most productive place—on the work itself.

What do you expect from me and am I falling short?

This can be a powerful question to ask of others, whether it's your peer, your manager, or someone who reports to you. It's far better to know that you're falling short of an expectation than to allow the situation to fester and create a communication gap or a split in the relationship. If you hear something you don't like, don't be defensive. If the stated expectations are unrealistic, you can always have that conversation.

Don't be afraid to engage in these expectations conversations. Though they can be uncomfortable at times, they're the best way to ensure that your focus is in the right place, and that there aren't any unspoken issues within your relationships. A known issue is typically less destructive than an unknown issue because you can confront it head-on rather than being blind-sided by it later.

The Fear Conversation

This is the most nebulous of the conversations and is one of the more difficult to get people to open up to, but it can be one of the most powerful if we have the guts to engage in it. The fear conversation is all about shining light into dark, unspoken places and neutralizing fear where it lives.

What are you afraid might happen, and why?

This is an especially powerful conversation to have in a team context when you are about to act on a new idea. There are typically unspoken fears at the beginning of a project, especially related to the potential for failure, and making the effort to call them out can help neutralize them immediately. Once you come to terms with the actual risks involved in a project, and you discuss the true consequences of failure, it will limit the role that fear plays in your creative process. However, if you allow your imagination to run wild and never discuss your fears in the context of your team, fear can cause self-limitation and unnecessary worry.

Similarly, you can engage in this conversation with a peer or a friend when you are embarking on a new project. Simply sharing your fear of a potential outcome and asking the other person to engage in that conversation with you can help you redefine reality and assess what's *truly* a risk versus what you perceive to be a risk. Sometimes we artificially escalate risk beyond its true bounds, and in doing this we may fail to fully engage in the work or take the risks necessary to do brilliant work.

What was the last risk you took?

Talking about risk is a great way to normalize it. Once we become aware of what others around us are doing in their pursuit of great work, it gives us courage to do the same. Ask others about the risks they are taking in their life and work, and then share yours. This will dispel the lie that you are alone in taking worthwhile, calculated risks, and will help you better assess the kinds of risks you should be taking in your work.

The Engagement Conversation

This conversation is about helping you identify patterns of energy and enthusiasm in others and tap into the deep well of inspiration around you. It will help you stay attuned to the perceptions of others and—especially if you are a team leader—help you keep a finger on the pulse of the organization's collective energy.

What's inspiring you?

This is a powerful question to ask others. It will help you discover what others are noticing, reading, watching, or otherwise absorbing that's firing them up. It's also a great way to identify things that you should add to your list of things to experience. Similarly, when you share what's inspiring you with others, you are forced to explain concepts and teach others about what you're seeing and noticing. The simple act of sharing it with others will often help you better internalize it and think of ways it applies to your own work. As has often been said, the best way to learn something is to teach it.

How do you feel about the work we're doing?

Thoughts and feelings are often very different. We might think that a decision is quite rational, but we are emotionally unattached to it. You get a very different answer when you begin probing for emotional responses versus rational ones. Emotions, however, are often the best in-the-moment gauge of the temperature of the team. You can change your thinking on a subject, but it's impossible to immediately change your emotions. Regularly ask others around you how they feel about the work, and take time to consider how you feel about it as well. Don't sacrifice emotional engagement on the altar of rational engagement.

What's the best thing we're doing and why?

Again, this is a great question to ask in a team context. (I often challenge leaders to use this question as a gauge of future leadership potential. If someone intuits that something is valuable, but they aren't aware that it's an organizational priority, it can signal that they are sharply attuned to the strategy and plans of the organization.) Ask others to share what they think is the best work being done and why, then share your thoughts on the subject. It's a great way to check alignment and have a discussion around team perceptions of the work.

The "Final 10 Percent" Conversation

In any conversation, there is always a final remnant—a "final 10 percent"—that is left unsaid. Thus, people often walk away having said most, though not all, of what they wish they'd said. These remnants don't remain unspoken, however. Instead, they often get shared in secret, and do damage to relationships when they turn critical or turn into gossip. It's far better to have these conversations directly between the relevant parties and keep them in the open rather than allowing them to become destructive. The "final 10 percent" conversation is about getting to the "final remnant" of feedback that others may not volunteer unless you ask for it.

What's something I'm doing that doesn't make sense?

Creating a culture of transparent trust requires that you be able to speak difficult truth to one another. Model this environment by asking people you trust to share what they see you doing that makes no sense to them. Not only is this an effective tool for self-awareness, but it also creates a culture in which others believe that you are willing to hear difficult or challenging things and act on them, which goes a long way toward eliminating judgment or the impulse to gossip. If people know they can say things in the open, it removes the felt need to say them behind closed doors.

What's the smartest thing I'm doing right now?

This is similar to the above question, only focused on the positive things people observe about your work. You're not fishing for compliments, but instead you are seeking reinforcement of your chosen priorities and a better understanding of how your work is being perceived within the organization. (Ask this question selectively and within the context of a trusted relationship, or it may come across as self-serving.)

What's something obvious that you don't think I'm seeing?

In the interest of self-awareness, ask someone to share with you something that they observe in your work that they don't think you see. Having eyes and ears on the entire context of your work can help you stay alert to perceived strengths, weaknesses, opportunities, or threats that you may be overlooking and can thus help you when you conduct your personal SWOT analysis.

How to Have the Five Conversations

These five conversations are best conducted in the context of both team and individual relationships. Do not steamroller others with them or awkwardly try to work them into small talk. ("Hey . . . speaking of music, what's the dumbest thing I'm doing right now?") Instead, set aside time for your team, with those you manage, or with your manager and peers to have in-depth conversations about *how* you're doing the work rather than just conversations about the mechanics of the work, which is where most teams exclusively focus. The better you get at these conversations, the more clarity, alignment, and energy you'll find in the work environment, and the better equipped you'll be to unleash your best work.

Do not treat your relationships haphazardly. Be intentional, and treat them as an opportunity to both serve and be served. Be generous, aggressively honest, and do your best each day to close any open loops.

Don't allow a lack of intentional effort to prevent you from emptying yourself each day of your best work. Engage your relationships each day in such a way that you'll have no regrets tomorrow.

CHECKPOINT

It's easy to close off from relationships when things get busy, but it's important to recognize that these are the exact times when effective collaboration is most essential. Collaborative relationships demand persistent work to help you to stay aligned, close loops, and clear the air of any misunderstandings.

Are there any open relational loops or areas of conflict in your life that need to be closed?

Is there any area of your work where one of the five conversations should happen today in order to bring alignment? Which conversation, and when will you have it?

Who will you connect with today, just to touch base and share your work?

Share this principle: Make it a habit to regularly engage in the five conversations with others. Don't make a production of it; just work them naturally into conversation. As you do, you'll find that they clear the air of a lot of tension, and help build trust and alignment in your relationships.

11

Live EMPTY

The foolish man seeks happiness in the distance;
the wise grows it under his feet.

—JAMES OPPENHEIM

There's a tense scene in the movie *Apollo 13*, based on the actual events of the near-disastrous Apollo 13 mission, in which three astronauts are stranded hopelessly in space and trying to make it back to Earth after a failed lunar landing. They have only a few minutes to fire the rockets on their space capsule to realign its course with their needed reentry trajectory. If they are even marginally off in their efforts, they will burn up in Earth's atmosphere, or bounce right off it and into space forever. Because they had insufficient power to activate their guidance system, their only means of checking the accuracy of their efforts was to keep the earth visible in a tiny window in the side of the craft. In the movie version of events, all is almost lost when the earth slips momentarily out of sight, only to suddenly reappear at the last moment, proving that their realignment was successful.

Navigating toward our objectives is very much like firing our navigational rockets, trying to stay in alignment while trying to keep the moon visible through a tiny window. It takes intentional effort and constant redirection, and without regular checkpoints it's easy to drift off course. We may be slightly off course much of the time, but if we are intentional, we will eventually get to our destination.

In this chapter, we'll systemize and concentrate on some of the questions in the Checkpoint sections at the ends of the previous chapters. You'll learn how to use them each day to ensure that you lay your head down each night with few or no regrets about how you spent your focus, time, and energy.

Why Daily?

Many productivity systems recommend reviewing work and priorities on a weekly basis. The practice I'm recommending is not intended to replace those weekly reviews or assessments, but to supplement (and complement) them. I often find that a week is too much time between minor readjustments, and the practice I'm recommending takes only about fifteen to twenty minutes a day, but can notably improve your focus, time, and energy management.

The goal of the daily checkpoint is to refocus on your effectiveness rather than your efficiency. In the midst of the hustle of daily work it's easy to lock down on tasks that give you an immediate sense of progress, such as responding to e-mails or returning phone calls, but sometimes the most effective activities fall to the side in the process. This means that some of the items that show up on your task list or calendar may not give you the ping of immediate progress on your projects, but they are increasing your capacity to do better work or improving your understanding of a problem you're trying to solve. In other words, they are meshing.

Of course, it's easy to confuse progress with effectiveness. All progress is not true progress. It's possible to gain ground for many days, weeks, months, or even years but be going in a completely wrong direction. That's why it's important to have mechanisms in your life to help you decide whether your efforts are, in fact, helping you advance on your goals, or just feeding your need for forward motion.

Remember that in order to do your best work, you must engage in Mapping, Making, and Meshing, including the subtle forms of each discussed throughout the book. The following process is designed to help you examine your life daily for areas where you might be slipping into stasis.

EMPTY

There is a five-step process you can follow to scan your life for potential action points, and position yourself to do work you'll be proud of later. While the approach described below is introduced in a work context, any and all of these questions can benefit you in any aspect of your life. It's impossible to truly separate your "work" life from your "personal" life, so there is little difference between the demands on your time from your

job or your family and friends. You still have only so many resources to go around, and you have to get good at how you allocate them. Feel free to adapt the process to fit your needs and
to help you gain traction on what matters most to you.

Set aside ten to fifteen minutes each day to perform a daily
checkpoint. (For those who are already doing a daily checkpoint recommended in *The Accidental Creative*, the concepts described in this chapter can simply be folded into that time, as
many of the concepts overlap.) The daily checkpoint is designed
to help you determine how you will engage your day, and to
predetermine how you handle any obstacles that arise on your
path to getting your best work out of you. The five-step process
follows the acronym EMPTY. Take out a fresh piece of paper or
open a new file and follow the exercises below.

E: Focus on your Ethics

In Chapter 7 you were challenged to develop a code of ethics
for how you will engage your day. Your code of ethics consists of
several words that define your engagement, your relationships,
and what specific aspects of yourself you will bring to your work
each day. Write the words that comprise your code of ethics on
the page, then do the following.

Look at today's appointments, commitments, and tasks. Take a
few minutes to look over your upcoming commitments. Review
everything that will require your focus, time, and energy today.

Consider how you will apply your ethic to each of them. As
you glance at your commitments, how will you engage them today? Will any of them require more focus, time, or energy than

the others? What can you do to ensure that you'll live out your ethic as you move through your day?

Consider potential pitfalls. Are there any items on your daily list that you know will present a challenge to your ability to live out your ethic? (Maybe an especially tense meeting, challenging relationship, or mind-numbing task?) Determine in advance how you are going to deal with these challenges when they arise. By doing so, you lessen the chance that those pitfalls will side-track you, because you will have a plan for dealing with them.

M: Focus on your Mission

As discussed in Chapter 4, so much of your effectiveness is about defining the battles that you know you need to fight, and directing your resources toward them. As you survey your daily commitments, ask yourself the following:

What change will exist today as a result of my efforts? Is there a step goal on the agenda for today? Determine now how you will know if your day was a success, and commit to working until you've achieved it. Be realistic, and recognize that big, long-term success is actually the result of a long string of daily successes. If you stretch yourself to win the smaller battles each day, then you will someday find you're making important progress on the larger fight. Focus on the right battles and the war will take care of itself.

What isn't already represented? What have you been meaning to do, but haven't made the effort to work it into your daily routine? Do you need to add a task, a call, or some other kind of action to your day? What do you need to start that you've been putting off?

What needs to go away? A big part of having a defined understanding of your important battles is knowing when things need to be moved off your plate. You cannot do everything at once or you will do nothing well. You must prune your life so that your most important priorities can have the focus, time, and energy they need from you. What needs to be removed from your lists today so that you can focus your attention on what's most important?

P: Focus on People

As mentioned in Chapter 10, your relationships are critical and are the biggest opportunity for you to add and receive value in your life and work. Take a minute to consider the relationships in your life, and specifically those you'll engage in today.

Who will you interact with today? Take a look at your calendar and your other commitments and think about each of the people you'll interact with today. For a brief minute, consider them, what you value about them, and any outstanding issues that may need to be resolved.

Are there any open relational loops to close? As you survey your daily schedule, do you see any opportunities to close open loops or engage in conversations that might help bring better alignment or clarity? Do you need to have any of the five conversations (clarity, expectations, fear, engagement, final 10 percent) in order to gain better understanding of the relationship or your work? Is there anyone you need to reconnect with or write a note to?

How can you serve others today? Again, as you think about the
people you'll encounter today, is there any way in which you
could serve them that would be unexpected or add a disproportionate amount of value? It's easy to allow relationships to slip
into autopilot, or to take them for granted. How could you surprise someone today with generosity or encouragement?

T: Focus on Tasks

This is the nitty-gritty part of your day, really. You make progress only if you engage with urgency and diligence in your tasks.
But sometimes the tasks that show up on your list aren't necessarily the ones that should be there. You inherit tasks from yesterday or turn your task list into more of a wish list.

Consider your daily priorities. What absolutely must get done
today, and when will you do it? If you're able, block off time on
your calendar to engage in your most important tasks so that
you're not trying to do them in the cracks and crevices of your
schedule. Dedicate specific time blocks to delve deeply into them
so that you don't have to stress and wonder when they'll get done.
This will free you up to be present in all of your other commitments today. Brilliant work demands dedicated time on your calendar.

Define your projects. It's impossible to solve a problem you
haven't defined, and yet many of us drift from day to day with a
vague sense of the projects we're responsible for without ever
stopping to truly consider the issues at hand. As you consider
the projects you are accountable for, take a few minutes to consider the problems you are still trying to solve. I realize that this

may sound a little obvious, but consider that the answers to those questions change frequently, sometimes as often as daily if you're making good progress. Simply take a few minutes to make certain that the problems you were solving yesterday are still the problems you're working to solve today. Don't get carried along by your work—define it, daily.

Y: Focus on You

In the fray of daily work, it's so easy to lose track of yourself. You can easily get caught up in checking things off lists and managing your relationships that you neglect to do the small but consequential things that lay the foundation for your future effectiveness.

What will you do today to develop yourself? Are you learning a new skill, tackling a passion project, or pursuing a specific curiosity? Will you take a risk to try something new? Commit today to doing something that will stretch you beyond your present bounds and force you to grow. If you do this daily, you will eventually find that the incremental stretching will add up to remarkable growth over weeks, months, and years.

What do you need to start moving on? Is there anything you're feeling a sense of urgency to start? Sometimes you have a nagging sense in the back of your mind that you should be doing something, but then the practical side of you kicks in and begins to edit your thoughts. "What if?" and "Maybe I should . . ." quickly turn into "That's not practical" and "You just need to focus on what's in front of you." Get started. Today's the day.

Be grateful. Take a few minutes to be grateful for your life. It doesn't matter how much or little you have, there are always things to be thankful for, and when you focus your mind on what you have rather than obsessing on all the things you lack, it has an amazing effect on your ability to be present in your day and pour yourself fully into your work.

Dream a little. If you have time left, spend some time dreaming a bit about what you'd like to see happen. In an ideal world, how would you spend your days, what kinds of opportunities would you have, and who would you interact with? Are there latent dreams or ambitions that you've allowed to fall to the side that you need to pick up, dust off, and begin acting on? Are there any items that you would add to the "before I die" wall that you've been neglecting because you simply didn't know where to begin? If something comes to mind every day as you engage in this exercise, then it's something to pay attention to.

Valuing the Process

"So, what do you do?"

It's a rational and relatively safe place to start a conversation. After all, many of us spend close to half of our waking adult lives engaging in and commuting to our occupation. If you want to know how someone spends a good portion of their time and energy, just ask them about their job.

What's interesting, though, is how people typically answer that question. They usually respond with a noun rather than a verb. With "I'm a . . ." rather than with "I . . ."

"I'm an accountant."

"I'm a manager at a retail store."

"I'm a writer."

The container for their work—the job—is given in response. But that job isn't the same thing as the work they do. It's just a handle to help contextualize the work for someone else. Your job is a collection of activities that allow you to add value to the world. Some of those activities add more value than others, and some disproportionately so. There are things that you can choose to do in the course of your day that help you accomplish your job, but are not necessarily indicative of the real work that you need to do in order to make a genuine and unique contribution. Your vocation often transcends your occupation.

It's very important not to make that same confusion when you reflect personally about what you do each day. The work that you do when you're actually working is very different from the set of tasks that you might accomplish. There is some set of activities that comprises your real work, and it is a subset of the activities you must do to meet your expectations and objectives. These activities are the ones that allow you to add a disproportionate amount of value compared with the others.

For example, there are a lot of activities that a manager must do in the course of her day. There are typically strategic decisions to be made, e-mails and reports to be processed, and relationships to be managed. However, a very small portion of those activities are the ones that will have a huge impact on the organization. These are the activities that make the manager effective, even if they seem immediately inefficient at the moment.

"It never feels efficient to sit and have a conversation about a decision I'm trying to make with a team member," one manager told me, "but I've come to learn that these conversations build strategic consensus within the team and help others feel vested in the decision-making process."

We need to fall in love with the process, not just the end product of our work. A writer writes regardless of whether he gets accolades. A designer creates order and meaning from chaos regardless of whether she is recognized. And an artist—of any capacity—makes his art whether or not he ever gets the raise or the corner office or the bigger platform to share his work.

Make sure that you're nurturing your process. It's the only thing you can truly control, and it's the thing you'll always have regardless of where you end up.

The best way to nurture and fall in love with process is by implementing these daily checkpoints to keep you doing the things that truly matter. By doing so, you will ensure that you have points of traction in the right places, and you will at least be making intentional decisions about what you choose *not* to do. When it comes to minimizing later regrets, intentionality and structure form the keystone.

12

Forward

People pay for what they do, and still more for what they have allowed themselves to become. And they pay for it very simply; by the lives they lead.

—JAMES BALDWIN, *GO TELL IT ON THE MOUNTAIN*

Remember paper maps? The kind that forced you to weigh the benefit of looking at the map against the time spent trying to figure out how to refold it afterward? Once upon a time, before many people began relying exclusively on GPS, if you were traveling in a strange area, you'd carry one of these with you in case you got lost. In my twenties, I spent a lot of time on the road, and I had a full atlas of the United States in my car. However, that atlas was useless unless I had two pieces of information: my location and my bearing. I couldn't just randomly open the atlas to a map and choose a destination without knowing where I was and in which direction I was facing. But once I had these two pieces of information, I could navigate to pretty much any destination.

In the age of GPS and turn-by-turn navigation, the subtleties of the art of map reading have become less crucial. You need to know only a single piece of information—your desired destination—and the technology does all the heavy lifting. Unfortunately, the GPS method of navigation doesn't work when plotting your life and work. You cannot get where you're going unless you understand where you currently stand, and in which direction you're already heading. As such, no advice—no matter how carefully crafted and lovingly offered—is universally applicable. You cannot follow someone else's map.

I believe this is why so many people feel frustrated and aimless when it comes to figuring out how they should engage in their work. They are swimming in advice and information from books, websites, or friends and colleagues about how to be more effective, yet they feel hopeless because it doesn't seem to apply directly to them. In a lot of cases, it doesn't. It provides hope of a more promising future, but that's it. In order for the advice to be applicable and helpful, it has to be translated to their situation.

This is the inherent problem with trying to imitate someone else's success. The steps they took to get to where they are, while perhaps instructive, don't provide a concrete action plan for you. You must figure out how to apply their map to your situation.

But this isn't what we wish for. We'd prefer a guaranteed method for success. We want the results without the uncertainty and risk. The hard truth is that there is no real and lasting success without the potential for failure. The pain of the journey is what allows you to sustain your success on the other side.

Throughout this book, you've been introduced to some of the most common areas where bright, gifted, hardworking people unwittingly get stuck. While there is no formula that can be applied to every life to provide the key to certain success, regularly scanning for the Seven Deadly Sins of Mediocrity is the best method I've uncovered for staying on an upward trajectory. It's not foolproof, however. It requires one additional element: drive. You can have the map, and there can be gas in the tank, but unless you're willing to fire up the engine and put your foot on the gas, you'll never get anywhere. Intention and theory don't change the world; decisive action does.

As such, this final chapter is a "gut check" to challenge you to really consider where you are in your work, where you'd like to be, and how you'll get there. What follows are some final thoughts on the nature of contribution to help you stay resolved to unleash your best work rather than settle.

What Does Life Expect of You?

In 1942, Viktor Frankl, a prominent Jewish lecturer and psychotherapist, was seized and placed in a Nazi concentration camp. Over the remaining years of World War II he was forced to deal with unfathomable acts of atrocity, and was stripped of every artifice of human dignity. Many members of his family perished in the camps, including his wife, mother, father, and brother, in addition to many of his friends.

During his experiences in multiple concentration camps, Frankl recorded observations of other captives and their varying methods of dealing with the atrocities thrust upon them. He noted that the captives who seemed to fare best were those who tended to ascribe a sense of meaning to their suffering. In other words, they had constructed a narrative that helped them understand not just what was happening, but also why it was happening, and how their ability to suffer well mattered in the deeper scheme of events.

Frankl managed to survive his internment, and after the conclusion of the war, he compiled these observations into a book later published under the title *Man's Search for Meaning*, in which he argued that the greatest source of the hopelessness, despair, and apathy that define the lives of many is what he dubbed the "existential vacuum." He described it as the sense of void that people experience when they don't understand the deeper purpose of their life. Frankl argued that when people seem to be drifting along, succeeding or failing with little sense of how or why any of it fits into the grander picture of their existence, they tend toward despair and depression. He wrote,

> What was really needed was a fundamental change in our attitude toward life. We had to learn ourselves and, furthermore, we had to teach the despairing men, that *it did not really matter what we expected from life, but rather what life expected from us.* We needed to stop asking about the meaning of life, and instead to think of ourselves as those who were being questioned by life—daily and hourly. Our answer must consist, not in talk and meditation, but in right action and in right conduct. Life ultimately means taking the responsibility to find the right answer to its problems and to fulfill the tasks which it constantly sets for each individual.

Frankl's admonishment that purpose and meaning are discovered not through excessive contemplation, but through action seems spot-on. To tap into your best work and to stay on a path of productive contribution over the long term you must commit to discovering that contribution by attaching yourself to an active mission. Rather than asking the question "What do I expect from life," you must, as Frankl indicated, ask "What does life expect from me?"

Stop *Trying* to Be Great. Just Be Great.

A friend once shared with me that his son was experiencing some paralysis about what to do with his life. He said that he sensed an intense pressure to try to do something great, and to really make a mark on the world. My friend paused for a moment, then turned to his son and asked, "How many great people can you name? Let's start with U.S. presidents. That's easy; there are less than fifty of them." His son was able to name several, but nowhere near all of them. After that, my friend asked him to list all the other great people he could recall. Finally, he had to jump in and help his son with the list. In all, my friend guessed, they could probably name close to a hundred people before it started getting really difficult.

"OK, so let's think about this for a minute," he told his son. "You can name about a hundred people throughout all history who meet your criteria of being great. Do you mean to tell me that you're making it your ambition in life to try to be number one hundred and one? Is that what you're going for?"

He encouraged his son to focus less on the perceptions of others and instead on finding an interesting field to work in, and to spend his energy trying to make a difference in the world around him. Don't worry about being great in the eyes of others; focus on excelling at your work.

The desire to be seen as great can be a paralyzing force. It's something you can't control. Measure your work by your daily progress on what matters to you, and leave the obsession with arbitrary scorecards to others.

Don't Give In to the "Lag"

If you survey the virtual landscape of the lives of many creative professionals (and organizations), you'll find it littered with fragments of ideas, half-finished projects, and abandoned inspiration. In truth, there is rarely enough time to do all the things we want to do, and some of these castaway projects are casualties of limited focus and time. However, there is something else at work that causes people to lose their steam and give up before they can reap the rewards of their effort.

I call it the *lag*.

The lag is the gap between cause and effect. It's the season between planting a seed and reaping a harvest. It's the time when all the work you've done seems to have returned little to no visible reward, and there is little on the horizon to indicate that things are going to get better.

When you are in the lag, the only thing that keeps you moving forward are (a) confidence in your vision and ability to bring it to fruition, (b) a willingness to say no to other things that tempt you to divert from your course, and (c) daily, diligent, urgent progress.

As discussed throughout this book, urgency and diligence are the foundation of "hustle," and hustle is the best antidote to lifelong regret. If you hustle, you never have to wonder "what if?" It's difficult to hustle when you're in the lag, because you experience all the pain with little return, but without the effort you won't get to experience the rewards.

To be clear, there's nothing wrong with quitting. In fact, there are times when it makes more sense to quit than to continue. However, quitting should be a strategic choice, not one made out of fear or discomfort. You should be moving toward something promising, not just running away from your lack of comfort.

Often, people give up during the lag and they subsequently fail to reap the reward for all their hard work. Don't forget that there is always a delay between planting and harvesting.

Optimism vs. Wishful Thinking

There's a vast difference between optimism and wishful thinking. One is a mind-set that expects progress through effort, and the other is nothing but a bulwark against the fear of failure.

Someone who is optimistic expects the best while actively working to bring it about. Wishing externalizes responsibility and hopes that everything lines up according to plan, but doesn't do anything to actively bring about the desired change. Someone who operates from a place of wishful thinking is—in essence—a closet pessimist.

To have an opportunity to excel, you have to put in the time to develop a platform that provides the kind of opportunities you desire. If you are wishing for someone to hand them to you, you will be disappointed. Rather, you must be willing to proactively do work that has no definite return, but that is an investment in your future. This is how the optimist functions.

As a core part of this optimistic operating ethic, you must alter your mind-set to be about making a contribution, consistently and daily, with a keen eye on how you are leveraging your unique aptitudes to add value to the world around you.

Chris Guillebeau is an entrepreneur and author of the book *The $100 Startup*, which encourages people to use the resources available to them to start something that adds value to the marketplace. In an interview, he told me that he believes the most important shift one can make is toward a mind-set of intention and purpose.

"How do people live their lives with intention and purpose? I believe they do so first by understanding their own motivations and aspirations. Why do we do what we do? What's the point? What are we working toward?" he said. According to Guillebeau, gaining an understanding of your personal motivations is critical.

Interestingly, Guillebeau argues that orienting your life around making a contribution—around meeting the needs of *others*—is actually the key to finding personal satisfaction. "I believe we should all focus on the core issue of contribution: What are we making or offering for the world at large? How are we engaging? I call this practice 'selfish generosity,' because as we seek to engage, we ourselves benefit. Most of us want to be part of something bigger than ourselves. As we seek to contribute, we ourselves are changed."

Redefining Success (and Failure)

Winston Churchill said, "Success is not final, failure is not fatal: it is the courage to continue that counts." When was the last time you failed at something? How did you know?

A lot of discussion takes place in entrepreneurial/creative circles around the subject of failure. There are some who argue that failure is a critical part of growth. Others argue that failure is overcelebrated, and the cultural obsession with "failing fast and failing often" is encouraging the wrong kind of focus.

I was recently watching a fascinating interview with Sara Blakely, the founder of Spanx and a newbie on the Forbes list of richest people. In the interview (and in the Forbes article) she says that when she was a child her father made it a habit to ask on a regular basis, "What did you fail at this week?" When she replied, "Nothing," he would retort, "Oh . . . that's too bad."

Of this ritual she says, "My definition of failure became 'not trying,' not the outcome."

Our definition of failure defines us more than we may realize, because fear of failure is one of the most frequent sources of paralysis. When the perceived threat of potential consequence outweighs the perceived benefits of success, we stop acting.

Notice the word "perceived." These consequences are often illusory, but in our mind they are as real as a tiger staring us down. The problem is that we can go for days, weeks, months, years, lifetimes without ever really getting to the bottom of this fear. The result is that we forfeit our best work.

Two things will paralyze our creativity faster than anything else:

1. **We haven't defined success.**
2. **We haven't defined failure.**

If we don't have a clear definition of what we're trying to do, we will spin out. Simultaneously, if we don't have a clear definition of "missing the mark," we will experience paralysis. The simple act of clarifying these two concepts can immediately yield courage for your work.

So I ask again: What did you fail at this week? How did you know?

Problem Finding vs. Problem Solving

In the past, successful people were typically those who were good problem solvers. They could take disparate bits of data, crunch them, and weave together an elegant solution to the problem. Over the next several decades, people who are especially adept at problem *finding* will define the world of work. These are people who are intensely curious and willing to apply their cognitive abilities to exploring the gray zone adjacent to existing opportunities until they identify a vein of gold.

Bob Lokken grew up in a rural Montana hamlet of about thirty people. He says that his time growing up there taught him to identify and solve problems, and to add value from a very early age. "I came to learn early on that the best way for me to be a part of something great was to find a way to add value to it. Everything else seemed to take care of itself."

Because of his recognition of those problem-solving aptitudes, he chose to study engineering in college and upon graduation he began to pursue his graduate degree, but was convinced to leave school in order to join a start-up. "I saw two paths in front of me. This was the 1980s, so I could go sit in a cubicle farm with hundreds of other engineers working for a defense contractor, or I could go the start-up route and be a part of something uncertain, but exciting. I chose the path where I thought I would see the entire span of a business, and learn as much as I could." After a few years with the start-up, he launched his first entrepreneurial venture inside of the company, giving him the chance to experience leading a start-up without the same measure of risk.

Lokken soon decided that it was time for him to launch a company of his own. He co-founded ProClarity, a business intelligence company, and served as its CEO for several years. Over a decade, the company grew dramatically and was eventually sold to Microsoft in 2006. After a successful exit, Lokken was in the situation many entrepreneurs dream of. At age forty-six, he was still young, had more money than he needed, and was pretty much free to do whatever he wanted with the rest of his life. "I spent a few months sitting around, playing golf, and doing all of the normal stuff you kind of think of while working eighty-hour weeks. My wife came up to me one day and said, 'You're not seriously just going to sit around and do nothing with your life, are you? It would be a shame for you to have learned so much from your other experiences, only to let that go to waste.' She was right, and I'd already been thinking the same thing."

Instead of spending time dreaming about what he might *enjoy* doing, Lokken instead began listing the big societal problems he thought he could affect. "I saw three big issues that were in real need of effort: education, energy, and health care. I'm not a physicist, so I immediately eliminated energy. I also knew that analytics weren't really a key solution for the education issues we are facing, but I still thought I could perhaps help in that area by lending my experience to schools and teaching."

That left only health care, and Lokken quickly assembled a team to begin thinking about how he might be able to make a difference. "Health care was massively complex and very interesting to me. I knew that the industry was in a time of transition, which made it a prime candidate for disruption. I love disruption. I'm bad at the top, but I'm really good at coming into an industry and figuring out how to shake things up. I challenged my team with 'Let's go see if we can do something significantly better than what's out there.'"

Lokken and his colleagues founded WhiteCloud Analytics, a company that provides valuable data services to the health-care industry. The company's goal is to simplify the process by which doctors make decisions in the treatment of patients, and to provide a better, data-driven backbone to the diagnosis and treatment process. "It is a big vision," Lokken commented, "but that's the place where we saw we could make the biggest contribution."

Lokken says that his philosophy about work has not changed much since his time in that Montana hamlet. "It's really all about trying to add as much value to the market as you can. I've learned from observation that the way people succeed is by adding a tremendous amount of value to the lives of others."

As Lokken stated at the close of our interview, "A mercenary mind-set tends to attract a mercenary crowd." Like Lokken, you must approach your work from the perspective of problem finding, and commit yourself to pouring everything you have into solving those issues. The future—your future—will be defined by those who choose to contribute more value than they consume.

Stay Off the Merry-Go-Round

I experience a lot of merry-go-round conversations in which someone expresses frustration about their work, their relationships, their career, and their life in general, but they're doing little to change the situation. They are waiting for their circumstances to change rather than actively taking responsibility. Then things seem to get better temporarily, but a few months later, here they come around again, complaining about the same issues. Another trip around the merry-go-round, but nothing has changed.

The truth is many of these people know what to do about their circumstances, but they're afraid to make decisions. Instead, they push the decision into the future, hoping that something will shift and that their world will suddenly be better. Before long, they've wasted days, weeks, months, or even years in stagnation, waiting and wishing for something more, but doing little other than complaining. Unfortunately, by the time they take action, their options are more limited.

I've frequently witnessed this in organizations, especially in people frustrated with their manager or career path. "I just wish I could have more opportunity" or "My manager is too controlling" or "There seems to be no future for me here" are common laments. They know what needs to be done, but they are deferring the discomfort of acting on their decision.

There are few things more uncomfortable and draining than resolving the right course of action, but lacking the courage to act upon it. As my friend riCardo Crespo frequently says, "You can't lie to the person in the mirror." When you know what to do, but lack the conviction of action, you risk too much. It becomes increasingly difficult to act over time.

When the right course of action is evident, we're forced to make a choice between following our convictions or ignoring them. If we ignore our convictions enough times, we eventually lose our sense of self. We can no longer hear the inner voice prompting us that we are capable of more, and that we don't have to succumb to mediocrity or settle for an unhealthy situation. Don't defer important decisions. Act now.

Stay Out of the "Gray Zone"

All great feats, whether building a business or raising a healthy family, are the result of alternating cycles of tension and release. Capacity and character are born and tested in the fertile fields of tension, where we are challenged to stretch to our limits, and then we recover through rest and reflection.

Think about how muscle is built. You have to strategically stress the muscle by pushing it to its limits, then allow it to rest, which is when the muscle fibers repair and grow. Over time, this alternating cycle of tension and release increases the capacity of the muscle. One personal trainer told me that the most dangerous place for someone wanting to get in good physical shape is what he calls the "gray zone." This is the place where you've developed the capacity to do a reasonable workout, but you're no longer stretching yourself beyond your comfort zone. You get the "ping" of a good workout, but none of the benefits that accompany strategic discomfort.

Similarly, a growing business will go through a cycle of chaos and tension, followed by the resolution of that tension when a business problem is solved, followed by more chaos/tension as the business tackles a new challenge, and so on. When the business stops stretching itself and seeking new challenges—when it gets stuck in the "gray zone"—it stops growing.

The reason individuals and businesses get stuck in the gray zone isn't always due to laziness. Sometimes it's simply because the comfort of what's known wins out over the discomfort of uncertainty. When faced with potential failure, our survival instinct pushes us to default to that which is most certain. You must embrace uncertainty as a part of the game, and be willing to take daily, measured action to confront it. The only two approaches to dealing with uncertainty are design and default. When you operate by default, your biology, which is wired for comfort, wins out and you almost always end up squarely in the gray zone.

You can spend many years in the gray zone, with the illusion that you're contributing, but knowing deep down that you're not really offering up your best effort. You're doing enough to get by, but nothing better. You don't have to settle. Respect yourself and your work enough to spend yourself fully on worthy problems. Don't allow complacency to rob you of years of engagement and fulfilling contribution. As the entrepreneur Rich Seal told me in an interview, "Never commit to anything that you can't give your all to. Hustle overcomes nearly every shortcoming."

Don't Hold Out on Us

When I was sixteen years old, I awoke one night unable to move my legs. I rolled out of bed and crawled with my arms to my parents' room across the hall, barely able to moan the word "help" because of the extreme pain in my lower back. My parents called an ambulance, and while the remainder of the night is a blur, I awoke in the hospital the following morning with a semicircle of family staring at me.

There was obviously something wrong, but none of the doctors could identify precisely what it was. All they could tell was that there appeared to be some sort of mass growing inside my lower abdomen. Cancer? Maybe. No one seemed certain, but the one thing they all agreed on was that the only way to find out was surgery. I was prepped, sedated, and wheeled into the operating room.

It turned out that the "mass" in my stomach was actually a swollen muscle. There was an infection growing in my abdomen, and the muscle playing host to it had swollen to the size of a softball. The muscle was pressing against a major nerve, which signaled to my body, "Hey, it's time to close up shop down here." Even after they discovered what was wrong, I was in excruciating pain for several weeks.

I spent close to two months in the hospital, lost nearly fifty pounds, and had to learn how to walk all over again. (It was later determined that the source of the infection was most likely my habit of licking my fingers in order to wet the bottoms of my high-tops to gain traction on the basketball court.) While in the hospital, I had a lot of time to think. Even as a sophomore in high school, I was beginning to ask myself where my life was headed. I spent a lot of time writing and listening to the radio to quell the boredom. Unfortunately, the radio in my hospital room would pick up only one station, which happened to be an adult contemporary station, and its most popular song at the time—which was played every hour on the hour—was "The Living Years" by Mike and the Mechanics. To this day, the final line of the chorus is etched into my mind: "It's too late when we die to admit we don't see eye to eye."

I remember reflecting at the time about how close I'd come to death. It seems silly—it was only an infection, after all—but there was a period of a few days where it seemed like many of the people cycling through my hospital room were hyperconscious of what they said. It was almost as if they wanted to ensure that their last words to me would be kind ones; that I would go out with a favorable impression of them.

I recall thinking, "When I get out of the hospital, I'm going to treat my life with more purpose. I'm going to act on the things that matter." I'd had my first major life epiphany: someday I'm going to die, and there's nothing I can do about it. I realized that all I could do was embrace the time I'd been given, and use it as best I could.

In the wake of my time in the hospital, I discovered a newfound sense of courage and began taking small, daily risks and forcing myself out of my comfort zone. I began writing songs and performing them for friends, something I'd never really done up to that point out of a fear of being mocked. I even began performing some of the music publicly. As I struggled to regain the weight I'd lost, I attacked physical conditioning with new vigor and committed to reclaiming my position on the basketball team the following season, something I'd been told would be next to impossible. (It wasn't, and I did.) My personal relationships improved, and I found a new kind of clarity in my schoolwork. I was finding my voice. It was almost like I'd been given a clean slate—a new beginning.

Why did all this suddenly begin to happen in my life? In large part, I think it was because of the epiphany I'd experienced in the hospital. I realized that I had a scarce amount of time and resources available, and I wanted to take advantage of my new lease on life. The narcissism of my teenage years was interrupted and replaced by a deep gratitude for life and mobility.

I wish I could conclude this story with a phrase like "and that's how I won the Nobel Prize" or "I made my first million dollars that year," but life rarely works that way. The small, personal, and seemingly insignificant battles I won over the course of those few months didn't alter world history, but they completely changed the trajectory of my life. They established a new vector for me founded in the realization that every moment and every choice is significant. They taught me to live my life with urgent diligence, and not to withhold making a contribution, regardless of how unremarkable it may seem at the time. That lesson continues to pay dividends more than twenty years later. I know that my contribution is defined by how I choose to engage the battles I face every day, and that my legacy is nothing but a series of choices to engage in or abstain from action.

I hope that this book has been helpful in some way in instilling a similar level of urgency in how you think about your life. You have a finite amount of focus, time, and energy to offer the world, and it can never be reclaimed once it's spent. There's no use in wasting your time lamenting the past, because you cannot change or control it. Rather, I urge you to focus on what's next.

Ultimately, your life will be measured by what you gave, not what you received. Don't hold out on the rest of us—we need you to contribute. Spend your life building a body of work you will be proud of. Engage today with urgency and diligence. Plant seeds every day that will yield a harvest later. Tomorrow is only an unfulfilled wish, so live and work as if today is all you have. If you do, you will be able to lay your head down each night satisfied with your work, and in the end, you will die empty of regret, but full of satisfaction for a life well lived.

ACKNOWLEDGMENTS

While writing is performed in isolation, it's never a solitary act. I'm deeply grateful to all those who lent their wisdom and effort to this book.

I'm grateful to those whose stories are featured in the book, or whom I interviewed during the writing process, including Lauren, David, Matt, Sarah Peck, Brian Tome, Jerry McLaughlin, Steven Pressfield, Peter Bregman, Seth Godin, Rich Seal, Chris Brogan, Loren Long, Sarah Young, Karen Ward, Jodi Glickman, Chris Guillebeau, and Bob Lokken. Thanks to Doug White and Rob Seddon for reading the early drafts and offering very helpful insights. I am grateful to Matt Chandler and David Valentine for encouraging me to write this book rather than a different one, and to Julien Smith for the "kick in the rear." Also, thank you to the many clients and audiences who let me share some of these insights while they were still in the formative stage.

Many thanks to my (brilliant) editor, Emily Angell, for her patience, for always having the red pen at the ready when I got off track, and for not holding back. Thanks also to Adrian Zackheim and Will Weisser for the freedom to write from my passion area and for adding some much-needed clarity at the eleventh hour. To Margot Stamas, Bria Sanford, Katie Coe, and the rest of the Portfolio team, thanks for their efforts in helping bring this book into being.

I continue to be indebted to my agent, Melissa Sarver, for the diligence and urgency with which she approaches her work.

Thanks to Les Tuerk and Tom Nielssen of BrightSight Group for helping me get in front of audiences to share my message.

Thank you to riCardo Crespo, Brian Tome, Steven Manuel, and Chuck Mingo for the continued encouragement and sharpening. Also, thanks to Matt Gartland and Mindy Holahan for valuable support.

Thanks to my clients and to the Web-community members who read posts, listen to podcasts, and offer invaluable feedback and encouragement.

Finally, thanks to my family, who had to bear the brunt of the stress of the writing process. Rachel, you are my ballast. Ethan, Owen, and Ava, may you live life to the fullest, contribute as only you can, and die empty.

NOTES AND SELECTED FURTHER READING

Throughout the book, several resources are cited. Below is a collection of references and recommended resources for further reading. Additionally, you can find many podcasts, interviews, articles, and more at AccidentalCreative.com and ToddHenry.com.

All the resources listed below can also be found at DieEmpty.com/resources.

1 Die Empty

The story of Candy Chang's "Before I Die . . ." wall can be found on her website (beforeidie.cc/) and can be heard through a talk she delivered at TED (www.ted.com/talks/candy_chang_before_i_die_i_want_to.html).

The Accidental Creative by Todd Henry discusses the dynamics of creativity in the workplace and offers practical methods for increasing effectiveness.

2 Your Contribution

You can find a full transcript of the Steve Jobs commencement address at Stanford at news.stanford.edu/news/2005/june15/jobs-061505.html.

The *State of Create* survey (sponsored by Adobe and conducted by StrategyONE) showing the attitude toward creativity in the workplace, at school, and at home can be found at www.adobe.com/aboutadobe/pressroom/pdfs/Adobe_State_of_Create_Global_Benchmark_Study.pdf.

Working by Studs Turkel provides an outstanding cross section of attitudes about work from people doing a wide variety of jobs.

The 2012 documentary *Searching for Sugarman* shares the life story of musician Sixto Rodriguez.

3 The Siren Song of Mediocrity

Herbert Simon popularized use of the phrase "satisficing" and was a prominent voice in the shaping the modern understanding of the decision-making process. As a starting point, you can learn more about him at en.wikipedia.org/wiki/Herbert_A._Simon.

The Innovator's Dilemma by Clayton Christensen reveals some of the forces that cause companies to stop innovating and the dynamics of how market disruption occurs.

The Monster.com "When I Grow Up" Super Bowl ad can be found at www.youtube.com/watch?v=myG8hq1Mk00.

Ann Patchett's commencement address at Sarah Lawrence College was later published as a book, titled *What Now?*

4 Define Your Battles

The full transcript of Curtis Martin's Hall of Fame speech is posted on www.profootballhof.com/hof/member.aspx?PlayerId=299&tab= Speech. A starting point for learning more about Martin is http:/ en.wikipedia.org/wiki/Curtis_Martin, which also features a weal of citations about his on- and off-field activities.

5 Be Fiercely Curious

The Shallows by Nicholas Carr is a valuable examination of the eff technology on our minds and thus our interaction with our er ment.

The Impact Equation by Chris Brogan and Julien Smith share into how to work with meaning.

Steal Like an Artist by Austin Kleon offers tips for living a mo and artistic life.

The List by Roseanne Cash was her album of cover songs the list her father, the legendary Johnny Cash, gave he

The Art of Innovation by IDEO founder Tom Kelley offer sights into innovation uncovered over the course of

The Power of Myth by Joseph Campbell (with Bill Moyers) features interviews with Campbell about the role of myth in everyday life.

6 Step Out of Your Comfort Zone

Sarah Peck's amazing story can be found on her website at itstartswith .com/2012/07/birthday-swim.

Dr. Karl Pillemer's interviews with elder experts was compiled into his 2011 book *30 Lessons for Living: Tried and True Advice from the Wisest Americans.*

The story of Jeff Bezos's regret minimization framework was shared in his induction speech to the Academy of Achievement in 2001. The interview and transcript are found at www.achievement.org/aut odoc/page/bez0int-3.

Oh, the Places You Will Go by Dr. Seuss is a classic for kids of all ages.

Poke the Box by Seth Godin challenges readers to act now rather than wait to be picked by others.

unts of Jerry Seinfeld's advice to Brad Isaac are widespread on the b, but one account can be found at lifehacker.com/281626/ seinfelds-productivity-secret.

Franklin's morning and evening questions, along with his irtues, can be found in *The Autobiography of Benjamin*

7 Know Yourself

even Pressfield is a wonderful and motivating read et fear squash creative pursuits.

8 Minutes offers excellent tips on personal pro- work with a sense of purpose.

nfidently Adaptable

ins articulates the five stages of decline

shares insights into how to add in-

9 Find Your Voice

The Artist's Way by Julia Cameron shares a methodology for reclaiming artistic passion and living life more creatively.

You can learn more about Loren Long's work at www.lorenlong.com.

The article in which Jad Abumrad shared the story of how *Radiolab* found its voice is at transom.org/?p=28787.

Anything You Want by Derek Sivers offers insights for aspiring entrepreneurs from his own entrepreneurial journey. His reflections on the importance of doing what's obvious can be found at sivers.org/obvious.

10 Stay Connected

The rock tumbler story is found in the film *Steve Jobs: The Lost Interview* by Robert Cringely. The edited clip can be found at www.youtube.com/watch?v=K-Yv-UdsmSo. A transcript can be found at tech.fortune.cnn.com/2011/11/11/steve-jobs-the-parable-of-the-stones.

12 Forward

Man's Search for Meaning is Viktor Frankl's account of his time in concentration camps and what he learned from the experience about the nature of humanity.

In *The $100 Startup* Chris Guillebeau shares practical tips for launching and operating a microbusiness.

The interview with Sara Blakely can be found at abcnews.go.com/WNT/video/spanx-entrepreneur-shares-advice-15889928.

INDEX

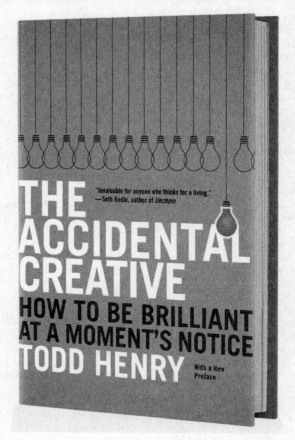